30 DAYS TO BREAKTHROUGH

Thirty Days to Breakthrough: Peace

www.inscribeministries.com

Published by: Inscribe
Editor and Creative Consultant: Jeffrey Pelton, www.jeffreypelton.com
Cover Concept by: SkyTree Productions, www.skytreeproductions.com

First Edition, 2015
ISBN-13:9781517596996
10 9 8 7 6 5 4 3 2 1

30 DAYS TO BREAKTHROUGH

Peace

Kathi Pelton

Foreword by Doug Addison

Dedication

This book is dedicated to my husband, Jeffrey. His name means, "God's Peace" and I have watched him reach for the peace of God relentlessly. He is not only my husband but my editor. Most editors correct punctuation, spelling and grammatical errors, and keep the book focused, but he makes every page more beautiful than I could ever imagine. He is far more a co-author than an editor. Thank you for your love and a life-long journey together into *PEACE*.

Acknowledgments:

Many people have believed in this project and sowed into seeing it published. We thank those who gave and prayed. You know who you are. This belongs to you! Special thanks to Karen Zheng. You helped us over the final hurdle.

Table of Contents

Foreword

by Doug Addison

This is a time of accelerated growth and in the midst of adversity God will bring breakthrough in our lives. The key to obtaining this is to develop peace. As we walk in perfect peace we activate spiritual principles that open the heavens over us.

Having peace sometimes does not make sense. The apostle Paul talks about having peace that transcends all understanding (Philippians 4:7). God's ways are usually higher than our own and His thoughts are not always ours. So a great way to discern God's voice is to look for the fingerprints of peace.

There is an attack right now to get people to worry, panic or become anxious. This is to try to keep you from operating in peace. Old things can come to the surface as God is bringing healing on a deeper level. Things are being brought to the surface for the purposes of strengthening you so that you can cross over into the new season at hand.

Recently, I had an angelic encounter in which I heard the Holy Spirit say that people everywhere need an impartation of peace and provision in order to rise above the storms happening right now. Whether you are aware of an angel or not, receive by faith that God is giving you new levels of peace and the resources you will need to get through this time of transition.

The opposite of peace is fear. Many people are being held down by a spirit of fear. A Heavenly remedy for this is to come into agreement with peace and not fear or worry. Fear can often try to disguise itself as wisdom. We need to understand the difference between fear and wisdom. When your decisions are motivated by fear you will not have a plan. When you are using wisdom, you will have heard from God and you will make decisions with divine intentions.

Operating out of fear can cause you to hesitate or hold back and possibly miss God's timing. There are times that you may need to use wisdom and put things on hold. But this usually comes with peace (not fear) and God confirms it with a plan or solution.

God is releasing divine solutions and it is not the time to hold back, but to move forward with confidence. Listen to God and look for peace to confirm it. Divine plans and strategies are coming to you now for how to get a radical breakthrough and not breakdown.

If you need to make a decision keep in mind that peace is the key to it all. Like Gideon we can be searching for confirmation on what to do next. Peace is the best fleece. As you learn to recognize God's voice and invite His presence into your daily life you will be in tune with the author of our destinies.

Get ready for a journey that will indeed change your life. This book is packed full of breakthrough strategies, powerful biblical principles and declaration prayers that will help you breakthrough to something new in the next 30 days!

Blessings,

Doug Addison

DougAddison.com

Doug Addison is a prophetic dream interpreter, speaker, writer, Life Coach, and stand-up comedian. Doug travels the world bringing a message of love, hope, and having fun! His unique style helps open people to discover their destiny and experience God's supernatural love and power. Doug releases *Daily Prophetic Words* and is the author of *Understand Your Dreams Now: Spiritual Dream Interpretation* and *Personal Development God's Way*. He and his wife Linda live in Los Angeles, California.

Introduction

Peace.

Deep within, every person craves it. We long for freedom from conflict and trauma; we grasp for security and pleasure; we desperately cling to anything that we believe will grant us the wonderful feeling of inner harmony and flood us with a blissful sense of well-being. Some of us look for peace through material possessions, or fulfillment in a career, or marriage and family, or seeking after all sorts of pleasures. We may work to create communities where individuals live in safety and tranquility.

We hope for peace; we dream of peace; we even fight wars to achieve peace.

And despite our best efforts, it seems more elusive than ever.

In a world afflicted and marred by constant chaos, some may feel that peace is unattainable. When challenging circumstances arise, a battle is played out in our minds: "What will I trust? Who will I trust? Is there anyone or anything that I CAN trust? How do I make sure I and my loved ones will be safe?"

We all have a natural tendency to search out ways to control our lives so we do not face turmoil. If we live free from the immediate threat of violent conflict, if we don't have to worry about hunger or homelessness, if we possess the resources we need to protect ourselves and our loved ones, we find it easy to live with a sense of peace. In our western culture, money is a powerful factor for most of us when we consider peace—or the lack thereof. Our family once went through a season where we had a substantial surplus of money in our bank account. We had no debt or unpaid bills. We could afford to buy more than simply our basic necessities. We had money for recreation. If sudden, unforeseen expense arose, such as a car that needed new tires or had an engine problem, we simply took it to our mechanic and had the problem fixed. We didn't lose peace because we knew that we had resources in hand.

But perfect peace is much more than simply a sense of peace. Our emotions are fickle, fleeting things, easily swayed by circumstances. True peace is a quiet, inner assurance that comes from knowing God cares for us and is concerned with all the details of our lives. Whether we are in abundance or in great need, we can experience the joy that comes from living in perfect peace.

There is a Hebrew word used in the Bible—*shalom*—that is usually translated as peace. But this word means so much more than our general concept of peace. *Shalom* derives from a root word denoting wholeness or completion; its frame of reference carries the notion of perfection. Thus, *shalom* is peace that has its source in God, and it conveys "peace, prosperity, health, completeness, safety....the state of fulfillment which is the result of God's presence....He is the one who will speak *shalom* to his people...." This marvelous word is a description of total well-being, rest and contentment. Countless people throughout history have experienced God's peace as they have refused to allow their lives to be directed by fierce storms of life raging about them, but rather looked with trust to their Almighty Creator and let His *shalom* be their guidance and strength.

God will be present with you in any storm you face, calming the waves of fear and confusion that threaten to drown you. He has authority over every earthly thing. Even though He does not promise that storms will not come, He does promise His perfect peace to calm you in the midst of the wind and the waves.

As we begin our journey, let us remind ourselves of the love and faithfulness of our Father, setting our minds and hearts on Him in trust and confidence that His ways are higher than ours, and He knows how to lead us to the path of genuine, lasting peace.

Day One

The Throne of Peace

As we stand together gazing at the path to peace, ready to cast worry aside and begin taking our first tentative steps, you may feel hesitant or fearful. Is it really possible to experience ongoing, calm assurance of God's care? The Bible clearly declares that our heavenly Father is powerful, merciful, kind and good, and He desires for us to receive all the good gifts He has for us, His children. Jesus told us to not be afraid, for it is the Father's pleasure to give us the Kingdom (Luke 11:32). He wants to impart to us His divine nature and holy character, but we must be rooted and grounded in His love, and be convinced of His authority to rule over every aspect of our lives. So, before we start walking, we will stop and talk about thrones.

Throughout history, men and women have sat on thrones as they ruled over nations, and their rule greatly affected the lives of the citizens. In the same way, there are characteristics in our lives that reveal what truly sits "enthroned" over our hearts. I have met people who are ruled by fear, control and pride. I also know people ruled by hope, intimacy and kindness. As we press in to know God, there is peace and rest available that serves as a garrison over our hearts and minds. As we give Christ Jesus His place on the throne of our lives, we will experience His rule and reign of peace. Peace is my gauge to what is ruling in my life. If I am not experiencing peace, it is a good sign that something is trying to move in and usurp Christ's reign in me, for when Jesus has the throne of my life I find that peace rules my heart. Hopelessness, fear, control and pride quickly flee when peace is ruling. Peace erects a strong fortress against those things that keep me from abiding in Him.

It is time for every believer to allow the Holy Spirit to search every aspect of our lives, and reveal anything that is not under submission to the lordship of our King Jesus. An important key to discerning areas that need alignment is to look at the places in your life that cause you the greatest anxiety. Most likely, those areas have not been fully placed into the powerful hands of Jesus. We all have those places, and there is no shame in that; but because of His great love, God is inviting you to kneel before the throne of grace and ask Him to align your life under His rule. He wants to purify you, so that the areas where you have lived with pain and fear can become fruitful fields of life fenced in by His peace.

When we know God and His peaceful rule, it sets us free from strife and fear. We are not subject to the winds of chaos and confusion that blow throughout the earth, but instead we have His abiding presence that leads us out of the belief systems of the world into the freedom of transformation. As we submit daily to His authority, in His Name we can command every negative thing that tries to usurp the throne of our hearts and lives to flee.

Daily Activation

Colossians 3:15

Let the peace of Christ rule in your hearts, since as members of one body you were called to peace. And be thankful.

Day One Declaration:

I declare and establish this day that only Christ Jesus can occupy the throne of my life. Jesus is the Prince of Peace and His peace can now have rule in my heart. I allow Him full authority to rule and reign in my heart and over every aspect of my life. I renounce every other force that has sought to rule my heart and I dethrone every other person or idol from the throne of my life. Thank you, Jesus, for coming to take your throne. Thank you for causing your peace rule in my heart and thank you that you have called me to peace.

Day Two

The LORD is Peace

Judges 6 recounts a difficult time for the inhabitants of Israel. They huddled in constant fear, hiding themselves from their enemies, the Midianites, who boldly ravaged them and stole their livestock, their crops and their peace. The promises of victory made to Israel during the deliverance from Egypt seemed to evaporate. Fear had become their way of life.

Can you relate to this? Do fear and loss seem to be the themes of your life?

At the time this chapter refers to, the Israelites had begun to worship at the altar of Baal. Baal referred to a Canaanite fertility god who was believed to produce crops and enable women to bear children. The word means "master," "lord" or "husband." Even though we say that we would never worship other gods, many still put their trust in jobs, investments, economic security, the safety of a strong government, and in their own ability to protect themselves and their loved ones. God asks us to tear down every "master or lord" that takes the place of trusting in the one and only true Lord: Jesus Christ. He is the One who gives us everything we need and the One who prospers us.

Fear and misplaced trust kept the Israelites from living in peace and prosperity. When God visited Gideon and revealed His plan to deliver His people, Gideon built an altar and called it, "The LORD is

Peace". The name of this altar became a powerful reminder for Israel, and it remains so for us as well.

When God spoke to Moses from the burning bush (Exodus 3:14-15), He revealed Himself as **YHWH ("I AM")**. In our western culture, we view names as identifiers, a way of explaining who someone is. But names in Hebrew thinking, as revealed in Scripture, are far more than labels of identification. They serve also to describe dynamic function; names explain not just who someone is, but what he is doing, and invite us into relationship. In this altar of Gideon, God revealed to us another of His glorious Names: **YHWH Shalom!** He is Peace; His Name is Peace; He is *our* peace! When we are oppressed and tempted to fear, we can run to our Father with absolute confidence and dwell with safety in the strong tower of this marvelous Name.

The name of ADONAI is a strong tower; a righteous person runs to it and is raised high [above danger] Proverbs 18:10 (CJB).

Yesterday we affirmed the lordship of Jesus over our lives. Today is the day to recognize and tear down every altar of trust you may have erected in the past to "other gods", even (especially) yourself! Ask the Holy Spirit to continue to show you any place that your trust has been in things other than Him. Let Him lead you through repentance and then allow your life to be an altar that bears His Name, "The LORD is Peace", for all to see.

Daily Activation

Judges 6:24

So Gideon built an altar to the LORD there and called it The LORD Is Peace.

Day Two Declaration:

I repent for every place that I have trusted in anything other than my Lord Jesus Christ. I break off everything that has been a master over my life and enslaved me to fear, robbery and lack. I tear down every altar of trust in carnal things such as money, man or my strength. I now return all of my worship and trust to Jesus alone. From today onward my life will be an altar that testifies that "The Lord is Peace" because He is giving me peace in exchange for all of my troubles and enemies.

Day Three

God with Us

The Gospel of Matthew tells us that before Jesus was born, an angel visited Joseph in a dream and told him that Mary would have a son, who would save His people from their sins. We know the story; we love to quote the familiar passage, especially during the Christmas season: *All this took place to fulfill what the Lord had said through the prophet: "The virgin will be with child and will give birth to a son, and they will call him Immanuel"--which means, "God with us"* (Matthew 1:22-23).

God with us! Three small words that contain a truth regarding abundance beyond anything we might dare to ask or think. It is one of the most beautiful and profound announcements ever given to mankind.

I once had a vivid dream about this promise that brought me great comfort during a time of sifting and testing in my life. In my dream, I was taken to a house where I met with a number of Christian leaders that I personally know. These leaders took me aside privately into a room and said that I had been brought there so I could pray and hear from the Lord on their behalf. Each of them was facing a significant crisis. One by one, each told me his or her concerns.

One lady explained that she had felt the Lord ask her to step out in faith and buy a house for ministry, but now she and her ministry were facing foreclosure on the house due to lack of payment. A married couple told me they had made a commitment to help orphans, but they were short of funds to fulfill their commitment. Another couple had just experienced the death of their youngest child, and they were praying in great faith for his resurrection, but were not seeing anything happen.

I felt overwhelmed by the responsibility to hear clearly for them, but could not turn away their requests to pray and see if the Holy Spirit might say something to me for each of them. I went into a room alone and began to call upon Jesus. Instantly I could feel keenly the anguish each of these precious people felt due to the magnitude of their problems, and I understood how viciously the enemy wanted to usurp their awareness of Jesus with doubt and pain, and with their overwhelming concerns. Then I heard what sounded like the audible voice of Jesus. He spoke one simple sentence: *"I am closer than any need you will ever have."*

The moment those words were spoken I became aware, more than ever in my life, of His nearness and presence. Every need that I ever faced and every question that I ever asked were suddenly unimportant in the light of His presence. For the first time, I felt as if I was experiencing and understanding the truth David knew when he sang *"The Lord is my Shepherd, I shall not want."*

It was as if I had no need or want of anything but His closeness and presence. The fearful needs that had so weighed upon me just moments earlier were utterly overshadowed by His presence. "God with us" was the answer. It was so simple, yet I have rarely experienced such calm assurance, such awareness of rest in

His faithfulness and incredible love. His presence filled me to overflowing with peace and abundance.

Today, ask the Holy Spirit to reveal the power of these simple words in your life. In my dream, I realized the words, without the experience, could sound trite and lacking in direction, but I knew that He would not speak without anointing and releasing His words to accomplish the same work in each person's heart as they had in mine. We have the promise from our Father that He spoke to Isaiah:

"For as the rain and the snow come down from heaven, and do not return there without watering the earth and making it bear and sprout, and furnishing seed to the sower and bread to the eater, so will My word be which goes forth from My mouth; it will not return to Me empty, without accomplishing what I desire, and without succeeding in the matter for which I sent it" (Isaiah 55:10-11).

We can put absolute trust in the promises our God has spoken. He demonstrates His faithfulness to us in the workings of our physical world; yet His spoken promises are even more true and sure than anything we can see with our natural eyes. Again, His presence is the calm assurance to our hearts that He is the abundant answer to our every need, whether now or in the future.

As I think back on how I felt during my dream, I am amazed at the experience of such absolute absence of worry and burdens. I didn't realize how much we carry upon ourselves that we were never intended to carry. Jesus told us in Matthew 11:28-30 (AMP):

"Come to Me, all you who labor and are heavy-laden and overburdened, and I will cause you to rest. [I will ease and relieve and refresh your souls.] Take My yoke upon you and learn of Me, for I am gentle (meek) and humble (lowly) in heart, and you will find rest (relief and ease and refreshment and recreation and blessed quiet) for your souls. For My yoke is wholesome (useful, good , not harsh, hard, sharp or pressing, but comfortable, gracious, and pleasant), and My burden is light and easy to be borne."

The words "blessed quiet" sum up what I experienced. All the stormy waves of need were calmed, all the bitter winds of questions were stilled. Every burden and sense of heaviness that had taken dominion in my soul were dethroned by His fullness. Jesus was given back His rightful throne as King in my life; every voice and need that had attempted to usurp His authority and love in my life were removed in that moment.

I still need to be reminded of His words regularly. Life has a way of pressing in on us with urgent, even frantic and chaotic demands. If we do not remain rooted and grounded in His love, remembering that "He is closer than my greatest need," it can be easy to fall into our old habit patterns of worry and striving to maintain control. As we continue to place our trust in Him and acknowledge His righteous—and rightful—rule and protection, we can experience the nearness of His presence and find comfort and restoration through His gentle and kind words and His profound presence and authority in our lives.

Today, let's declare again our trust in His presence. He is with us; Jesus is "God with us" and His presence brings peace.

Daily Activation

Psalm 118:6-7

The LORD is with me; I will not be afraid. What can man do to me? The LORD is with me; he is my helper....

Day Three Declaration

I declare this day that you are closer to me than my greatest need! Although my needs press in on me violently, Your presence brings calm and draws me into perfect love. I have everything I need in You. Just as the rains water the Earth and produce life, Your Word and promises of peace will surely produce life. Your words over me are not void but creative and full of life. Your presence is my peace and your promises are my provision. I lack no good thing because I am intimately known by You. Every detail of my life is covered and every need has the seal of Your love upon it. Today I stop carrying the burdens and the details of life's demands and enter into the peace of Your presence. I seek You first knowing that everything else will be added to me. You are closer than my greatest need! That is my truth and that is my peace this day.

Day Four

Peace, Not Fear

Do you long for this *shalom* we have discussed, the perfect and abundant peace only God can provide? It is an amazing experience to stand in the onslaught of adversity and remain in a state of peace, able to think clearly with your heart at rest. Peace changes everything.

Our world is engulfed in a continual, cosmic war that affects every living person, whether we are aware of the conflict or not. The Bible speaks of malevolent spiritual beings—satan and the demons—that hate humanity, since we have been created in the image of God. Jesus described this bitter enemy of all that is good as a thief who seeks to "steal, kill and destroy" (John 10:10). Much of the warfare that we face from day to day is waged against our peace. Anxiety and fear are weapons the thief uses to rob us of joy and intimacy with God and with other people. Anxiety and fear surround us with hopelessness, creating their own vortex of despair, just as a wildfire can create its own wind. On the other hand, peace brings freedom and makes room for joy and intimacy. True joy is found in the midst of true peace; a life lived apart from peace is a life lived separated from joy.

Peace creates an atmosphere of blessing, but fear creates an atmosphere of warfare. The Holy Spirit spoke to me one day and said, "*Fear is like bait for demons. They smell it and they gather to it in order to feast on its many delights. It gives strength to demons and leaves its victim weak and vulnerable.*" He went on to say, "*Peace is absolute confusion to the enemy. He doesn't recognize it; he cannot work within the atmosphere of peace because chaos and peace cannot coexist. Peace is the pathway to the banqueting table that I've prepared for you in the presence of your enemies. Peace is to fear like light is to darkness; it dispels it."*

This was one of the greatest revelations that I have ever received. The majority of the warfare that I've faced in my life has come from lack of peace. The loss of peace increased my warfare, because fear came in and the enemy had an atmosphere that he could breathe and work in. As I have allowed Holy Spirit to take me into deeper levels of peace I have found that it is an atmosphere of breakthrough. It is as if peace creates a portal that bypasses the enemy's opposition and connects us with greater perception of God's love and clarity regarding His purposes and will for us.

The devil and his demons thrive in an atmosphere of fear, but angels minister in an atmosphere of peace. Today God offers you a divine exchange. Jesus triumphed over all sin and wickedness and every dark plan of the enemy through His sacrifice on the Cross; He rose and lives forever in glory and victory and will graciously take your anxiety and fear, exchanging it for His peace. That peace can become the foundation of your life; then you will not be shaken.

Daily Activation

Jeremiah 17: 7-8 (AMP)

[Most] blessed is the man who believes in, trusts in, *and* relies on the Lord, and whose hope *and* confidence the Lord is. For he shall be like a tree planted by the waters that spreads out its roots by the river; and it shall not see *and* fear when heat comes; but its leaf shall be green. It shall not be anxious *and* full of care in the year of drought, nor shall it cease yielding fruit.

Day Four Declaration:

I am a man/woman of peace. I believe, trust and rely fully on the Lord and my hope is in Him alone. I will be like a strong tree with my roots firmly planted in the living water of Jesus Christ. I am at peace in times of abundance and in times of drought. I am fruitful and full of life. I declare that today I allow the peace of God to be the foundation of my life. I do not give way to fear; I do not accept its torment nor will I dwell in its foul atmosphere. Rather, I will breathe the pure fresh air of trust in my faithful Lord. As He establishes peace in my life, joy will be given a place to thrive. Today is the beginning of my journey of a life lived immersed in the peace of God.

Day Five

The Spirit-Controlled Mind

What controls your mind? Is it your flesh or the Spirit of God? The mind that is controlled by the flesh is subject to all the reactions and distractions of the flesh. Anger, lust, selfish ambition and envy are just a few of the traits that fill the mind that is governed by the flesh. Peace, purity, preference of others and love are traits that are enjoyed by the mind that is governed by the Spirit of God.

In the years before I knew Jesus, I had an understanding of right and wrong, but did not have the control of the Spirit to help me make the right choices. The desires of my flesh were always ruling my mind and my decisions. When I gave my heart to the Lord and began to allow His Spirit to control my mind, I found that I was led by peace. No longer did I react to life but rather I responded to life through the peace that the Holy Spirit gave me. However, it did not happen all at once, but took time and deliberate surrender to His will each day.

As a child, I had grown up with some awareness of God, but it was not until just after my eighteenth birthday that Jesus got hold of my heart and I committed my life to Him. He graciously led me to a wonderful fellowship, with a vibrant and loving group of young adults. I had dated continuously during my teenage years, since I craved comfort and security, and thought I could only find it through relationships with boys. This lifestyle had caused me a great deal of trouble and shame, so to be surrounded by young men who were following Jesus and seeking to live pure lives was refreshing and liberating. I began to establish friendships with males based on respect and trust, not simply physical attraction.

And the Holy Spirit was jealous to protect this work He was doing in me.

Late one summer morning, I was at a local community college, preparing to sign up for fall semester classes. I stood in line behind a nice looking young man, obviously about my age, and I struck up a conversation. It quickly became apparent that he was interested in me, and I was flattered by his attention. I could tell he was not a believer, but he was attractive and quite responsive to my flirtations. Right away, I sensed God's "still, small voice" inside warning me to stop—and stop immediately! But I was enjoying myself, and this guy was interesting, and handsome, and funny, and he didn't have a girlfriend and he was asking me to go out and what harm could come from one date anyway?

My flesh was singing an old familiar song, but disrupting the melody was a prompting from God that became more insistent. Clearly, He was warning me NOT to go out with this boy. In my foolishness—and, because I so interested at that moment in my own desires—I ignored the inner witness and tried to pretend I was just making it up. I convinced myself God would not object to my actions.

I was about to learn that I belonged to a heavenly Father who not only loves me, but He has quite a sense of humor. Since I seemed determined to ignore His quiet voice, He decided to speak loudly. Just as the young man smiled and asked me what night we should get together, I took a breath but before I could answer, a large flock of birds flew overhead, and released a deluge of "blessing"—right on my head! It splattered my shoulders, ran down my face, and spotted the front of my shirt. I shrieked with disgust, and my potential suitor stood silent, dumfounded by the display. Red-faced and sputtering, I hurriedly excused myself so I could go home and clean up.

I walked to my car, and before I could get in, the Lord spoke clearly—again—and said *"You belong to Me, and I will do whatever it takes to be sure you know that you are Mine. I want your whole heart and affections."*

Message received. I asked forgiveness, and promised God I would listen next time.

The Holy Spirit is a continual fountain of peaceful wisdom that He offers freely to us, and He invites us to enter into the process of receiving understanding, that we might learn to more fully walk in His ways. It requires effort, but the process is worth our attention. We are to be humble and teachable, which saves us a great deal of trouble. David gives wise counsel in Psalm 32:9: *"Do not be like the horse or the mule, which have no understanding but must be controlled by bit and bridle...."*

As I continue to ask Holy Spirit to govern my mind, I am able to walk in true repentance and my mind is renewed day by day. As my mind is renewed, peace increases to touch every area of my life. I am continuously freed from every thought that does not conform to the ways and the will and the holiness of Christ. It is a daily walk, requiring dependence on His grace and wisdom. But He gives peace, and by His grace, I am learning not to need bit or bridle—or flocks of birds!

Daily Activation

Romans 8:6

The mind governed by the flesh is death, but the mind governed by the Spirit is life and peace.

Day Five Declaration:

I declare that from this day onward my mind will be governed by the Holy Spirit! My mind belongs to You, God, and my thoughts will be transformed by your Spirit. Because my mind is now governed by your Spirit I will walk in life and peace. My flesh will not control my mind and lead me on the path leading to death, but I will walk on the path of life where your Spirit leads. I reject the governing and control of my flesh and receive the governing and control of your Spirit. Thank you for this realignment into peace.

Day Six

Peace in our Weakness

Often, many of us make the mistake of trying to use our own strength to obtain supernatural outcomes in our lives. At Mount Sinai, God gave mankind His laws of life (Exodus 19:16—24:4) and yet all human attempts to fulfill those righteous requirements have failed. Paul wrote in Romans 3:23 that *all have sinned and fall short of the glory of God* and he spoke to Peter and others gathered in Antioch, reminding them that we *"...have put our faith in Christ Jesus that we may be justified by faith in Christ and not by observing the law, because by observing the law no one will be justified"* (Galatians 2:16). We are saved by grace, and it is a gift from God (Ephesians 2:8-9).

The same is true of peace. Our attempts to gain peace will end in failure, just as our desire for right standing with God ends in failure, *if* we try to accomplish them with our own strength.

2 Corinthians 12: 9 says it best: *But he said to me, "My grace is sufficient for you, for my power is made perfect in weakness."* God is the One who will do for you what you cannot do for yourself. Do you feel as though you keep crashing into your own weakness and inability to help yourself as you seek to remain close to the Lord and live in His peace? It is by surrendering your weakness to God that He will come in and manifest His strength on your behalf. Our culture tells us that we should be strong and capable, but the world's insistence upon "freedom" through self-dependence simply reveals our fear and frantic

need for control, which ultimately leads to bondage. It is vital that we learn to become absolutely dependent on God, for in our dependency and weakness, He reveals His strength, which grants peace.

We have entered a time where God is patiently and deliberately extending the invitation to His sons and daughters to live in the safety and refuge of His strength. The process first exposes our greatest weaknesses and the areas where we have been living independently from His strength, exercising our independence through self-protection, striving and insecurities. Exposure can feel painful, but it is a gift from our loving Father, who calls us to surrender our strength and turn in humility to Him who is very present to scoop us up into His strong and loving arms and embrace us.

Peace is a gift of grace. Often, significant supernatural events happen in an atmosphere of human weakness and surrender. God's power is made perfect in these moments. It seems contradictory to feel peace and weakness simultaneously, but the reality is that that His power is released as we boast in the fact that it is "not I, but Christ" who brings me victory and restores my peace. He is never weak or lacking in power, and He makes the impossible possible.

Today is the day of surrender to peace even in the midst of your weakness, so that His power may be displayed. Let your faith arise as you face each day, because God's strength and power comes to do for you what you cannot do for yourself. He will be your peace.

Daily Activation

Micah 5:4-5

And He will arise and shepherd His flock in the strength of the LORD, in the majesty of the name of the LORD His God. And they will remain, because at that time He will be great to the ends of the earth. This One will be our peace.

Day Six Declaration:

I accept and declare that I cannot obtain peace by my human strength. I invite the One who is my peace to come and manifest His power and strength in the midst of my weakness. God will arise triumphant over my human weakness; He will reign despite my inability to overcome anxiety, fear and doubt. The strength of the LORD will be my help and my victory. He will be my strength and my song of deliverance. I declare that my weakness has now become an invitation to see His strength come forth.

Day Seven

Breaking Every Chain

God's intention has always been for you to live free from every chain that binds you and robs you of peace. Chains of fear, chains of shame, chains of sin and chains of anxiety are not God's plan for your life.

There is power in His name to set you free from every chain that hinders you from experiencing the peace that you were created to dwell in. Do not settle for anything less than peace and freedom. Bondage to sin and fear create an atmosphere of strife and chaos; the freedom purchased by Jesus brings peace.

As a girl, I was a victim of sexual abuse by a man who lived several months in our home. Due to this, many years later, unhealed pain from the abuse surfaced and I struggled with an eating disorder. I was married and already involved in ministry and leadership, so I was afraid to tell anyone—even Jeff—for a long time. Anyone who has ever been in bondage to an addiction knows the desperation, the shame, the torment that grips you continually. You know that the Bible says God will forgive and cleanse from all unrighteousness, but sometimes you feel shackled by darkness too deep for His light to penetrate. Eventually I confessed to my family and close friends, and I was helped greatly by trained counselors and by precious brothers and sisters in my local fellowship. They loved me, prayed for me, and stood by me, helping me to choose life instead of death.

But despite their support, I continued to face a desperate struggle. Night after agonizing night, for many grueling months, I would beg God to let me feel His presence, that I might be comforted and freed from my chains. During that that "dark night of the soul," I could identify with Jacob wrestling with the angel. I would fall, ask for forgiveness and deliverance, and say over and over "I will not let You go unless You bless me!" Sometime in the dark stillness of each early morning, the Holy Spirit would grant me enough peace so I could sleep, and I would awaken a few hours later with the resolve to continue another day, and face another night of desperation, crying out to Him. It seemed like a brutal process, but when my time of breakthrough came, it was sudden and dramatic and I was released into an experience of His manifest presence unlike anything I had ever known or imagined. I was given new eyes to see Him, new ears to hear Him, and awareness of His power that was breathtaking.

So, why didn't God simply reach out His hand and heal me quickly by His sovereign power? Why did I have to struggle so many months grasping at hope, gasping for breath, choked by the iron hand of my pain and weariness?

I came to discover that the deep wounds of betrayal and violence in my past had created such emptiness within me that the void had been filled thoroughly by lies: lies about people, lies about my own identity, and lies about the goodness and love of God. Jesus wanted me to experience the full extent of His mercy and His intimate care. Men in my past had simply wanted me for their own purposes. But God is not a man; He does not lie or seek us selfishly. He wasn't interested in just waving His hand over me to "fix" me so that He could display a nice, cleaned up little trophy of a healthy Christian woman. He wanted *me*—the real me—in all my pain and shame and howling despair. He proved to me that He would journey into any and every place of darkness within me, and by His gentle power and love walk me out into His light, where I would dwell in wholeness, and purity, and peace. He did not minimize the years of destruction I had endured; He showed me that He had taken it all upon Himself when He died on the cross, and through His triumph He led me into the strength of His freedom. He had not only breathed into me the breath of life; Jesus had also instilled a fearless confidence in His goodness toward me and trust in His desire to set me free from every enemy.

If you are aware of areas in your life where you are bound by chains, ask the Holy Spirit to set you free. Our God is no respecter of persons; He provided a specific pathway for me so I could walk in the freedom Jesus provided on the cross. This particular path ministered God's tenderness and wisdom in such a way that my heart was brought into profound trust and peace.

Jesus has provided for your freedom as well, and has a way of healing for you. Always remember that He loves you more than you can imagine, and His mercy is beyond your ability to fully comprehend. These words from A. W. Tozer are a potent reminder: "We must keep in mind...that the grace of God is infinite and eternal. As it had no beginning, so it can have no end, and being an attribute of God, it is as boundless as infinitude." The staggering immensity of God gives us hope in His grace and redemption that is far greater than any bondage.

Agree with the Holy Spirit that He is present now with His mighty power to deliver, and refuse to accept any form of bondage in your life. Ask Him if there are any actions you need to take, and believe that your Lord is on your side, willing and able to give you freedom from everything that enslaves you. He will never leave or forsake you, no matter how great your darkness.

Today is the day to move deeper into peace as you recognize that you are not enslaved, but free!

Daily Activation

Acts 21:7

And suddenly an angel of the Lord appeared [standing beside him], and a light shone in the place where he was. And the angel gently smote Peter on the side and awakened him, saying, Get up quickly! And the chains fell off his hands.

Day Seven Declaration:

Just as the angel of the Lord went to Peter to set him from of the chains that bound him, I too, am being set free from every chain that binds me. I will no longer be bound by fear, anxiety, shame or sin. Jesus has provided for my freedom and I accept His invitation to live in peace. I was created to live a life of peace and freedom. Today I enter into the freedom that my God has provided for me.

Day Eight

"But God..."

We made it through the first week! I hope you are beginning to understand more deeply the goodness of our Father, and find reasons to trust His kind intention to free you so you will more fully experience His love and peace. Peace is always available to you. It is available at all times and in every circumstance. This does not mean that it will not occasionally seem overwhelmingly difficult to maintain a feeling of peace; but when this happens, remember **YHWH Shalom** (The LORD is Peace) who promises to never leave or forsake you.

You may awaken from sleep troubled by a list of demands that need to be accomplished in your day. You may not have the means or the time to complete that list. Your work place has demands, bill collectors have demands, people around you have demands. How can you have peace in the midst of the clamor?

You may be in the midst of terrible physical or emotional pain, or suffering through a desperate situation in your life or the life of someone you love. How do you find the strength and hope you need?

There is an answer. *"But God..."!* In every situation, in every difficult demand, we have a "But God..." invitation. Because He lives in you, the negative declarations of your circumstance are not the final word. Read the Book of Psalms. David laments over his trials and sometimes despairs of his very existence, but he always finishes with a "But God..." declaration of truth. We continually read of him expressing his faith and sure confidence that he would stand in victory over all that was against him. He trusted even in the midst of conflict that the very joy and blessing he longed for would one day be his as he placed his trust in God.

Joseph was a young man with tremendous potential. He was dearly loved by his father, Jacob. God gave him dreams that clearly indicated he was destined for greatness. But, in his youthful zeal, Joseph unwisely shared those dreams with his older brothers, who responded with jealousy and hatred, selling him into slavery. Because of his good character and many talents, Joseph rose to prominence in his master's household, only to then be unjustly accused of attempted rape, for which he was thrown into prison. He continued to face obstacles of neglect, alienation, ingratitude, and loneliness during his long imprisonment. This life, initially so bright with promise, seemed to have descended into degradation and waste.

But God...! In the Lord's perfect timing, He suddenly catapulted Joseph from prisoner to ruler; he became second in command of what was at that time the most powerful nation on earth. Joseph was able to declare the wonders of God's purposes, as he told his brothers *"You intended to harm me, **but God** intended it for good to accomplish what is now being done, the saving of many lives."* (Genesis 50:20). Nothing happens in your life or my life that God cannot use for His purposes.

In his long years of imprisonment and rejection, Joseph learned to trust his life fully into the care of the One who does all things well. He did not dwell in self-pity or mourn lost opportunities; he realized that God had a purpose for him, no matter how his circumstances appeared. If you are facing an impossible situation, or find yourself in the middle of turmoil, don't end your day with lament; instead, release your "But God..." declaration. This will allow you to lay your head down in peace at all times and in every circumstance.

Daily Activation

Romans 5:8

But God demonstrates his own love for us in this: While we were still sinners, Christ died for us.

Psalm 73:26

My flesh and my heart may fail, but God is the strength of my heart and my portion forever.

1 Corinthians 1:27

But God chose the foolish things of the world to shame the wise; God chose the weak things of the world to shame the strong.

Day Eight Declaration:

I declare that no longer will I finish my days with declarations of defeat. I will honestly share my frustrations and the reality of what I am facing with God; then I will end my lament with a "But God..." declaration. I will no longer define my life by defeat and lack; instead I will define my life with the truth of God's goodness and faithfulness. Peace is with me at all times and in every way. I invite the Lord of peace to rescue me from every place that pain and distress have come to define me. I receive His peace right here and right now. I declare His peace to come upon every place of adversity in my life at this very moment. The Lord of peace is my help and the restorer of my life.

Day Nine

Living in the Moment

Do you live each day thankful for this "day the LORD has made"? Or do you spend most of your time either dwelling on your yesterdays, or dreaming about your tomorrows? The days of your past are past, today is the tomorrow that you dreamed about yesterday, and you do not know what the future holds. Your present moment may not look the way you envisioned, but nonetheless it is here and it is now.

When I was dating Jeff, he loved to take me on long drives to discover new sites. Often he would stop suddenly to point out moments of beauty; such as the way the sun was shining through a tree. I appreciated his constant attention to the moment, but in my youth I felt impatient to get to the destination. Then one day, the Lord spoke to me about my focus on the destination by saying, *"Don't miss the beauty of the journey. True living happens in the moment that you are in. That is where you find grace, strength and peace."*

Dreaming of tomorrow is wonderful but not at the expense of missing the moment. Worrying about tomorrow will cause unnecessary and fruitless striving and anxiety. The Word of God says not to be anxious about tomorrow, but to live in the day because there is only grace for today. Corrie Ten Boom wrote: "Worry does not empty tomorrow of its sorrow, it empties today of its strength." We can't pay tomorrow's bills with today's currency.

Another place we find our peace stolen is regret from the past. Sometimes we pass through a season of hardship or traumatic events, and even though we can look back and recognize the grace that God provided to carry us through, we relive the difficulty in our minds. The enemy is quick to whisper lies that say we will never recover or be restored. Like Lot's wife, we look back at the wake of devastation, rather than forward at the hope that lies before us. Lot's wife looked back, and became a pillar of salt. When we succumb to a spirit of fear, it is like being frozen in one place. But Scripture declares we have not been given a spirit of fear, but of power and of love and of a sound mind (2 Timothy 1:7).

Too often we become burdened and overly focused on our responsibility to be diligent and care for all we have been given. While it is true that God would have us be wise and humble stewards, it isn't "responsible" to worry and fret and fuss and try to order our lives so that they run as smoothly as possible. We are told to lay our worries and cares at the feet of Jesus and trust Him for our daily needs. I have experienced greater peace in my life as I've learned to truly experience the moment that I'm living in.

If you find yourself burdened with regret from your past or anxious with potential cares of tomorrow, take a moment to get back into "this moment" and realize your Lord is with you, wanting nothing more than intimate fellowship with you. Let all other concerns go as you trust in your Beloved. Lift your heart in worship and thank Him for His love and peace available to you right now, this moment. Embrace the day, enjoy each moment and love those who are next to you.

Daily Activation

Isaiah 55:12

You will go out in joy and be led forth in peace; the mountains and hills will burst into song before you, and all the trees of the field will clap their hands.

Day Nine Declaration:

Today is a gift from you, Father. I will embrace every moment, I will look for beauty, I will love the one in front of me and experience the journey of today. Today prepares me for tomorrow. I will go out in joy and be led forth in peace. I will rejoice in this day and be glad in the midst of it. I let go of anxiety about tomorrow and invite your perfect peace to immerse this day. My steps through the day will be ordered by you even as I have made my plans yesterday. I declare that this day is a day of grace and beauty.

Day Ten

Peace in Your Promise

About two years into our marriage, Jeff and I decided it was time to begin to try to have children. We had discussed it often, and were both eager to become parents, as we dearly loved children. We were full of dreams and rejoiced with the anticipation of excitement and wonder that comes with a new life.

I did not get pregnant right away. Still, we were confident that the time was right, and that this was a gift our Father wanted to give us. Scripture clearly told us that children are a blessing from the Lord. We were a little surprised and disappointed when conception did not take place right away; however, we were consoled by reminding ourselves "this often takes a few months."

But the months quickly began to add up, and still I was not pregnant. Time and again, I would hope, only to have my expectation crushed with the pains from my monthly cycle. Eventually, months turned into years; years filled with doctor visits and various tests and increasingly bitter disappointment. I longed to have a baby and could feel the hope almost as a physical presence, but our childless home continually reminded me of the empty ache in my heart. Eventually, the anguish turned into numb despair and hollow resignation. All of my friends were mommies—many with more than one child. I rejoiced with them, even as I wept in secret and wondered why I was not allowed the same joy.

Eventually, my doctor told me that it looked as though I may not be able to conceive. But God had promised me a baby! I had received much prayer from others, and I had prayed diligently myself. In those times of seeking, I would hear the whisper of Holy Spirit reminding me of His promise, encouraging me to be at peace.

Years passed, and I was not at peace. I was sad and depressed and tormented with doubts. I thought perhaps I had not truly heard from God; that maybe I was fooling myself with my own desires and would have to be content with a childless life. It seemed my husband and I would have to live without this particular "blessing from the Lord."

Then one night I had a dream that I gave birth to a baby girl. I held her in my arms and my heart filled with love and joy until I thought it would burst. When I woke from the dream, reality crashed in and I was broken and crushed with a new depth of despair. Now, it was as though I had a daughter and lost her. That day, I wrote in my journal about the joyous beauty of the dream and the bitterness of waking up to another day feeling empty and cold.

What I didn't know—and in my pain, couldn't have imagined—was that on that very day the baby girl that Jeff and I would eventually adopt had been born. My promise had been fulfilled, even though all I was aware of were my empty arms.

Sorrow and fear stole the joy of the words God had repeatedly spoken to me. I had actually given birth to the promise, but because peace did not rule in my heart, I missed the hope I was meant to receive through the dream given by my gracious Father. In His time, He brought us a blessing we could not have imagined. We not only received our little girl, but during the adoption process, I became pregnant with our first son.

Our Father is good. He is faithful. He is merciful. He understands the struggles and disappointments of life, and the anguish that can torment us. In the midst of our pain, He will remind us—if we listen—that He Himself is our fulfillment and our peace. Allow Him to fill your heart and give joy to every promise that you have received but not yet held. No matter the circumstance or the pain, He holds us still.

Daily Activation

1 Kings 8:56

Praise be to the LORD, who has given rest to his people Israel just as he promised. Not one word has failed of all the good promises he gave through his servant Moses.

2 Thessalonians 3:16

Now may the Lord of peace himself give you peace at all times and in every way. The Lord be with all of you.

Romans 4:20-21

...Abraham...was strengthened in his faith and gave glory to God, being fully persuaded that God had power to do what he had promised.

Day Ten Declaration:

I declare this day that the peace that makes room for the promises of God to be enjoyed in my life has come upon me. I embrace the peace that comes through faith, hope and love. No longer will fear and doubt steal the joy and expectation that come when God speaks a promise over my life. Today I will begin to enjoy the journey of being pregnant with promise. I will not miss the beauty that grows from the soil of peace. I will dream, I will rejoice and I will have peace that every promise that He has spoke to me will come to pass. I will have joy because I have peace and I will have peace because I have Christ.

Day Eleven

Peace in the Midst of Pain

The birth of my first child was very long and hard. I wanted to experience "natural childbirth" so I asked my doctor not to administer any pain medication. During labor, Jeff set up a stereo to play peaceful music, as I held his hand and breathed in and out during contractions. Or at least that was how it started. My labor pains increased, and increased, and after about thirty hours of labor I told Jeff to "turn off that annoying music" and stop telling me to breathe in and out! I had given up on peace and began to fight against every contraction. The next ten hours were horrible.

The next time I gave birth, I remembered my lack of peace in the midst of the pain during my first labor. This time I invited the Holy Spirit to help me embrace peace though the pain. Though I again experienced much pain, I was able to overcome it and work with it. The labor time was more than cut in half. I am convinced that the peace I invited helped my body to more readily give birth to our daughter.

Pain hurts, and often hurts badly! Sometimes we find ourselves suddenly in the midst of suffering when we thought we were about to enter into victory. Trusting God with our pain—even when He could have prevented the pain, but didn't—can be incredibly difficult. We must remember that God does not cause bad things to happen. Troubles come because we live in a fallen world; but God is the Healer of our pain and our broken hearts. *"The LORD is near to the brokenhearted, and saves those who are crushed in spirit. Many are the afflictions of the righteous; but the LORD delivers him out of them all"* (Psalm 34:18-19).

Recently I spoke with a person who had faced many agonizing setbacks in his life. His wounds were very deep, and although he greatly loves the Lord, he was finding it difficult to see beyond the pain and wondered if his life was always going to be defined by loss. Later, as I pondered my conversation with him, I realized that in Christ, losses and gains are very different than for those who have not found their life in Him.

> *...whatever things were gain to me, those things I have counted as loss for the sake of Christ. More than that, I count all things to be loss in view of the surpassing value of knowing Christ Jesus my Lord, for whom I have suffered the loss of all things, and count them but rubbish so that I may gain Christ, and may be found in Him, not having a righteousness of my own derived from the Law, but that which is through faith in Christ, the righteousness which comes from God on the basis of faith, that I may know Him and the power of His resurrection and the fellowship of His sufferings, being conformed to His death; in order that I may attain to the resurrection from the dead* (Philippians 3:7-11).

What losses can be compared with the gain of knowing Him and being found in him? This doesn't mean that we will not feel pain when losses come, but we are comforted by the true perspective that through it all, we have the great gain of knowing Him. Nothing can take this away from us; nothing and no one! Paul's magnificent declaration in Romans 8:38-39 is that *"...nothing can ever separate us from God's love which Christ Jesus our Lord shows us. We can't be separated by death or life, by angels or rulers, by anything in the present or anything I the future, by forces or powers in the world above or in the world below, or by anything else in creation."*

This profound truth is bedrock for our hope and trust during times of pain. The love of God will carry us through this life, even through the painful times. We can trust Him with our turmoil and suffering because it cannot separate us from His love. Jesus will meet us in the most painful places and comfort us with His love. I personally find His love to be most keenly felt in the midst of painful times. It is as though He wraps His love around us like a blanket and holds us near. If today you find yourself in pain, allow Him to wrap you in His love and comfort you. He is very near.

This world does have trouble and pain but God offers us peace in the midst of the pain. Fighting it only increases the pain and extends its duration. Today ask the Lord for the overcoming peace that is given to us by the One who has overcome the world.

Daily Activation

John 16:33

"I have told you these things, so that in me you may have peace. In this world you will have trouble. But take heart! I have overcome the world."

Day Eleven Declaration:

I declare the love and peace of Christ Jesus over my life that gives me victory. Christ is in me and He has overcome the world; therefore I am overcoming all of the trouble and pain that I face from living in this world. I have peace because I have victory through Jesus. I declare that I will embrace peace in the midst of pain that I face. I declare that I will not give up peace in times of trouble. Through Christ I will overcome in peace. I will birth God's promises for me and overcome every trial through the overcoming power of Jesus Christ. The song of my life will be peace and I will breathe peace in and out throughout each day.

Day Twelve

Be Still

One of my favorite times as a parent was those moments when I was alone with one of my babies while they slept in my arms. In the stillness of the house and the peacefulness of the child something would settle in upon me that felt like a warm blanket of love and comfort.

I often wonder if when we sleep God comes and holds us near and enjoys the peace of our stillness. I have been a foster parent to two babies that were born to drug addicted moms. A drug baby is rarely at peace. When they are awake they have to be swaddled, paced with, bounced and they almost never relax in your arms. It was only when they slept that I could snuggle them. Those were such sweet times of bonding and loving them.

God must experience the same thing with His children. We are so restless, rigid and rarely yield to intimacy. Our restlessness stems from our lack of peace and our lack of peace stems from a lack of trust. We believe Jesus will forgive our sins, but when it comes to needs in our daily lives, we live as though we think He will leave us short-handed. God has proven His faithfulness again and again, but we still question His faithfulness and look for ways that will give us control over the unknown. Unfortunately, many of us still demand that God prove Himself to us by tangible manifestations and fulfillment of our needs and desires. We require some sort of physical token to give us hope and grant us peace. But if that was the way God worked, there would be no need for faith. Our Father reaches to us and asks us to trust Him and be still.

Whether or not you had a trustworthy or loving father during your childhood, I can assure you that you have a trustworthy and ever-present Daddy in Heaven. Psalm 9:10 states: *Those who know Your name will trust in You, for You, LORD, have never forsaken those who seek You.* Your Heavenly Father cannot lie and He will never in any way abandon you. If you watch a small child with a good and attentive daddy, they are at peace. They do not go to bed wondering if they are safe or whether or not they will be clothed or fed the next morning; they just know that their daddy has all that they need. The same should be true with us.

God will accomplish all that needs to be done in your life as you enter into His rest. Richard Foster wrote: "This quiet rest…is not due to the absence of conflict or worry. In fact, it is not an absence at all, but rather a Presence. This peace is interrupted often by a multitude of distractions….But no matter—it is still there, and it is still real. And in time its quiet way wins over the chatter and clatter of our noisy hearts." His ways are not our ways; if you are taking matters into your own hands because you are afraid as you survey your natural circumstances then you will leave the place of rest and enter into striving. You will begin to trust your ways and your wisdom over His promises and His power to make a way for your miracle. This is not the way of faith. His ways may seem foolish to your rational mind; His leading often takes us in directions contrary to the "wisdom" of natural man. But follow the voice of your Good Shepherd and you will accomplish more than you ever thought possible through striving or natural wisdom. And you will have the joy of knowing you have honored Him!

His pleasure is not in the strength of the horse, nor his delight in the legs of a man; the LORD delights in those who fear him, who put their hope in his unfailing love (Psalm 147:10-11).

Seek first the Kingdom of God and His righteousness and everything else will be added to you. In His Kingdom, there is perfect rest. Did you have to strive to make the sun rise this morning? God is the One who holds everything in place. If He can hold the Universe in His hands, do you not believe that He is capable to hold your life and your concerns in His hands? Only do what He asks you to do and do it in rest. To be still does not mean to be motionless; it simply means that when you move, you move in peace.

Surrendering the fight to maintain control is vital to gaining peace. Will you rest in His love and be still in His arms? He's inviting you into the comfort of His peace and the security of His Fatherhood.

Daily Activation

Psalm 46:10

Be still, and know that I am God....

Day Twelve Declaration:

Today I let go of the fight for control in all the areas where I still struggle. I declare that your faithful love and nurturing care is over my life. I will stop fighting your affections and be still within your embrace. I will surrender my will to your peace. Flood my soul with peace, still my restless mind with truth and comfort my emotions with your love. You are God and therefore I can be still and be at peace.

Day Thirteen

Peace upon Your Family

When I was a young mother with four small children in tow, one of the greatest compliments I could receive was when some stranger would stop me and compliment me on how well behaved and peaceful my children were. What people didn't know is that our oldest daughter, whom we adopted, was born with fetal alcohol syndrome and drug exposure. She had multiple neurological disorders that would easily cause her to anything but peaceful. She was constantly inquisitive, but generally her focus wasn't on what we adults wanted her to focus upon! This created obvious problems with a traditional school setting, because her mind was over stimulated by all the busyness of a classroom. Sometimes we thought that her body carried enough energy to power a small city.

We nicknamed her "Hugger" because she loved to run into our arms in the midst of her play and get a tight hug. During those hugs I would often take a moment to pray peace upon her. It helped greatly with her ability to learn and retain information, because peace created an environment where her busy mind could take things in at a pace that worked for her.

Both doctors and teachers wanted us to medicate her so that she would pay attention, and we tried it for a while, but ultimately realized that medication stole her personality and joy. So, prayer and peace became her "medication." She grew up happy and *peacefully* energetic, and we have always been blessed with this wonderful and fun gift to our family.

God loves families! He created the idea of families, and is passionate for us to experience and display His character and goodness through this beautiful earthly expression. Our good Father cares deeply for every family unit on earth, and each member within those families.

As a mom, I find it hard to believe that anyone can love my children more than I do. I carry them every moment in my heart, in places too deep for words to express, but recently, I experienced deep revelation how much more powerful is the Father's intense love for them. I was praying for one of my sons who faced a terribly painful circumstance, and suddenly I was engulfed in the depth, the width and the height of the Father's love for him. It so far exceeded any love I have ever felt that I was completely undone. Of course, I have always known this was true in my mind, but experiencing it was beyond what I could have imagined.

As believers we "know" a lot of things about our Heavenly Father, and we believe those things. But sometimes we just need to stop and let ourselves experience His love. I am sure that what I experienced for my son that day was merely a shadow of the depths of God's love. If He had allowed me to experience more I do not know that my emotions or earthly body could have handled it. I was absolutely undone by the wisdom of His love, the kindness of His love and the burning passion of His love.

Sometimes I think we forget how incredibly emotional our Heavenly Father is. In this encounter, God was deeply emotional about the pain this son we share was enduring, and He wept through me with sobs that left me wrecked by His love and tenderness. His longing for our son to know His goodness and peace was beyond anything I previously comprehended. The Holy Spirit's desire to reveal the Father's heart and love roared within me like the sound of a violent storm or the crashing of waves in the ocean. As humans, often try to quiet or suppress our emotions and calm the deep expressions that we feel; God has no such restraints. He unashamedly wept and poured out His heart with such force that it left me unable to do anything but fall on the floor and weep with Him.

This experience has shifted how I see the love of the Father for me, for my family, and for every person that I encounter. Our Father does not hold back the great love He has for us. I sometimes wonder if it is His love for us that makes the seas rage, the winds blow or even the ground shake. We are loved with a power that shakes the heavens and the earth, and this love is a strong garrison of peace for us if we run together as a family into the strength of His arms.

As you go through your day today, ask the Father for a new awareness of His love for you and your family that is greater than anything that you will face or any fear that will try to cause you pain. His perfect love casts out fear and grants us overcoming peace! Nothing in heaven or on earth can stand against this awesome force. This day, declare the blessings of *shalom* over your family and your household. Let peace fill your home as you and your family dwell together, confident and secure in the great love of your Father.

Daily Activation

Isaiah 32:18

My people will live in peaceful dwelling places, in secure homes, in undisturbed places of rest.

Day Thirteen Declaration:

I declare this day that my home and my family will begin to come under God's canopy of peace. I will daily pray for peace upon every member of my household. I will pray for peace upon my life so that when we embrace I can impart peace to them. I declare peace over my home and say that it will be a place of rest; a peaceful dwelling place. With Your help, God, I will give my family a daily dose of peace, like a daily vitamin. I, too, will take peace into my soul and spirit each and every day. I will live in peace and train up my children (natural or spiritual children) to live in peace. I now declare peace upon my family!

Day Fourteen

Receiving the Good Report

In Numbers 13 we read about men who were sent to spy out the land of Canaan that God intended to give Israel. Some of the men came back with a bad report about the giants in the land, but two of them returned speaking of bounty—fruit, milk and honey in the land.

If God were to send spies into your life, would they bring back a bad report or a good report? I guarantee they would come back saying that your life has the potential for bearing bountiful fruit. Are there giants occupying areas of your life? Possibly, but God can conquer every giant and possess every part of you! This is your good report.

Have you believed a bad report about your life? There is power released when we believe the enemy's bad report. It stops the life and breath of God from flowing and it creates doubt and fear. God's report gives life and creates faith and peace. Let His report be the capstone of your life.

One day Jeff and I were on our way home from church, and we stopped to fill our car with gas. As Jeff got out of the car to pump the gas I saw a man on a big motorcycle pull up to the pump behind us. I noticed that he was tattooed, wore a leather vest and rode a Harley Davidson. He looked like a pretty rough guy.

As immediately as I noticed his rough appearance I also felt a strong quickening of the Lord to get out and speak to him. I knew that the Holy Spirit had a message but had no idea what it was going to be. Trusting that He would fill my mouth, I got out of the car and began walking toward him. I saw that Jeff was shaking his head. He told me later he was thinking, "What on earth is she doing?"

The man had just begun pumping gas, and I introduced myself and told him I was a Christian, and that I believed God wanted to say something to him. (I still had no idea what I was going to say!) He agreed to listen to me, so I took a deep breath and opened my mouth.

The words that came out sounded like something God would say to a believer. I kept speaking, even though I started to doubt if these words were at all accurate. I expressed to him how much the Lord loved his heart and his commitment to follow Him. Then I began to say that Jesus wanted him to know that he did not have to worry about all the mistakes of his past regarding his children, because God was going to heal his entire family and make all things new.

When I was done, all I could think was, "Wow, was that ever wrong! There is no way that this man is a believer."

I was wrong all right, but only because of my unbelief. The man's eyes filled with tears, and he began to tell me how he had recently given his life to the Lord, and just that morning had been baptized. But while he was riding home a heavy burden for his family came upon him and he felt overcome with sorrow because of all the pain that he had caused his family and wondered how those wrongs could ever be made right.

When he began to fill his bike with gas he felt a wave of despair come upon him due to all of the sins of his past. At that very moment I walked up to him and began to share with him what the Lord was saying.

I was as amazed as he was and peace flooded both of us. Where the enemy had come in to steal the joy of his salvation and the blessing of his baptism, God rushed in to restore his peace and hope for his family. And, in the midst of my doubt and embarrassment for possibly getting this word so wrong, God rushed in to teach me about walking in the confident peace of His abiding love. He gave us both a good report, speaking to us of the bounty of His goodness.

Today you can reject any bad report! Do not hesitate. God can turn your life around, your marriage around, your children around and even transform your city and nation when we align with His good report. There may be giants that have plagued you in the past, but before you lies bounty—fruit, milk and honey. God will give you victory as you put your trust in Him and focus on the fruit. He is able. Receive your good report and enter into His rest of peace.

Daily Activation

Numbers 13:30

Caleb silenced the people before Moses and said, "We should go up and take possession of the land, for we can certainly do it."

Philippians 4:8

Finally, brothers and sisters, whatever is true, whatever is noble, whatever is right, whatever is pure, whatever is lovely, whatever is admirable--if anything is excellent or praiseworthy--think about such things.

Day Fourteen Declaration:

God, today I declare that every good report that you have spoken over my life is the report that I receive and I believe. I reject every bad report spoken over my life or agreed with about my life. I cancel every negative word that I have spoken or agreed with concerning who I am or what my future holds. I now announce and decree that I am fruitful, blessed, favored and loved and I walk in overcoming victory. My life will be full of the fruit of the Spirit, full of His presence, full of victories and full of love. Christ overflows within me and I am becoming a bountiful and beautiful believer.

Day Fifteen

Prayers for Peace

Whenever I hear a Christian say that they are not an intercessor, I immediately think two things: one, they are missing the main key to their life's work and calling and two, they don't really know what an intercessor is. The word intercessor is defined *as a person who intervenes on behalf of another, especially by prayer.*

God urges us to pray for others; especially for our leaders and for those in authority. We are urged to pray for those in government, leaders in our schools and businesses, church leaders and even for parents. Positions of authority are seats of great responsibility. Tremendous burdens are placed on those in leadership and peace can be hard to maintain. We are told to pray for the peace of those in authority.

We read in the book of Nehemiah that as the people of Israel worked tirelessly to reconstruct the walls of Jerusalem that had been broken down, they faced tremendous opposition from their enemies. In this day, we are seeing a rebuilding of walls around God's people, and we are also seeing great threat and opposition. We must continue to rebuild and realign our lives. Christ is to be the Head of all that we do.

The times we live in are critical for the watchmen and gatekeepers to remain at their posts on the wall. A call is going out for families and individuals to hear God, find their place, and begin to work there. The enemy always goes through holes or gaps in our walls. This is true in both the spirit and the natural realms.

The enemy schemes and looks for gaps in the walls of our nations, our lives and the Church. Therefore, it is vital that we remain anchored in peace, and from that sure foundation we learn to pray the mind and the will of the Lord for ourselves, as well as for our leaders. Our enemy constantly attempts to threaten and deceive people, attempting to drive them to make decisions based on fear, instead of waiting to receive wisdom from the Lord. If you read the Book of Nehemiah, the threats were the same. But God gave Nehemiah strategy, strength, courage and success.

As we pray for those in authority, it truly causes nations, cities and structures to shift. We are given a marvelous opportunity as well as tremendous responsibility to bless those in authority with peace and the mind of Christ. Many leaders are unrighteous, and we do not bless their unrighteous acts or decisions, but we can call for the righteous will and purposes of God to prevail. Critical and judgmental statements against authority merely release agreement with the enemy against our leaders.

Read and reflect on the words of Paul below. If we want to live peaceful lives then heed God's urge to pray for those in authority.

Daily Activation

1 Timothy 2:1-4

I urge, then, first of all, that petitions, prayers, intercession and thanksgiving be made for all people—for kings and all those in authority, that we may live peaceful and quiet lives in all godliness and holiness. This is good, and pleases God our Savior, who wants all people to be saved and to come to a knowledge of the truth.

Day Fifteen Declaration:

I declare that I am an intercessor and as an intercessor I will pray for all those who are in authority. I release both salvation and the knowledge of truth upon those in authority in throughout the nations. I pray for the salvation of kings, prime ministers and presidents. I pray for the knowledge of truth to come upon leaders in the body of Christ. I renounce all negative words and judgments that I've harbored or spoken against those in authority. I pray now for their peace and their blessing. I declare godliness and holiness upon my life and upon the lives of those in authority in every sector of life. Thank you for those that you have place in authority and thank you that I can intervene on their behalf through prayer.

Day Sixteen

Peace through His Word

When my kids were young we always had fenced yards. This was to provide them with great freedom without sacrificing safety. They could run and play within the fenced yard and I had the peace of mind knowing that they would not be harmed.

I sometimes wish that God had a fenced yard so that I could clearly see the boundaries of safety that I can move within; but the truth is He does! It is His Word. The Bible reveals God's love to me, inviting me into greater intimacy with Him, and gives me instruction on how to live, giving me freedom to move within those boundaries. His Word also tells me that I will gain *great peace* as I live according to His commandments and His Word.

My part is taking the time to know His Word and His part is the promise of great peace. It is like having an invisible fence that gives me absolute freedom to enjoy this life along with the reward of a life marked by peace. He is such a wonderful Father. He has assured us that we will have everything we need to obtain peace by listening to, and obeying, His Word and His Spirit.

We have been given great and precious promises in the Bible. Through meditating upon them, believing them and trusting every aspect of our lives to the faithfulness of the One who made them, we grow in faith, in wisdom, and in peace. We learn how to filter the voices around us that clamor for attention, and hear the wisdom that comes from heaven. By that wisdom, we are able to sow peace and harvest righteousness (see James 3:17-18).

As we grow in peace, we hear ever more clearly this voice of wisdom. Peace calms the inner storms and noise produced by fear, allowing us to hear the counsel and wisdom of the Lord. Out of the whirlwind He spoke to Job: *"Give heed, O Job, listen to me; hold your peace, and I will speak. If you have anything to say, answer me; speak, for I desire to justify you. If [you do] not [have anything to say], listen to me; hold your peace, and I will teach you wisdom"* (Job 33:31-33 AMP).

If anyone had a reason for fear and anxiety it was Job, yet he was counseled to enter into peace and quiet so that he could learn wisdom. God's counsel and wisdom are the answers that we need. It is very difficult to be taught wisdom as we are tossed about on the sea of our anxious thoughts and words. This truth and exhortation is for us: *"Quiet yourself in My peace so that I may teach you wisdom."*

If you are lacking peace, take a moment to ask your Father if there is any area that you are not walking in His ways and commands. He is so faithful to put us back on the right track and return us to a place of peace and joy.

Daily Activation

Psalm 119:165

Great peace have those who love your law, and nothing can make them stumble.

Day Sixteen Declaration:

I declare this day that I will live within the boundaries of your laws and commandments. I love your law and I love your grace. I will quiet my heart and meditate upon Your Word, listening as You speak counsel and wisdom. It is by grace that I will fulfill all that you ask. I find safety and freedom within your gates. I receive the reward of great peace because I love your teachings. I will not fall if I will obey your Word. I will take the time to know your Word and your will. May your peace and love fence me into the safety of your will.

Day Seventeen

The Path of Peace

We live in a world marked by unrest, wars and chaos. How do we find a pathway of peace through the midst of it all? Our path of peace is found not in the natural world; it is in the realm of the spirit. It is the trail we decide to travel each day, one that runs counter to the headlong rush to destruction on the broad path of the world around us.

Even though we desire peace, and can—and should—pray for peace for the world around us, we do not have to wait for all chaos and confusion in our circumstances to cease. We can walk on a road of personal peace today. A highway of holiness and peace was made available to us the day we received salvation. No longer were we walking in the futility of our own thoughts, relying on our own strength; our spirits were made alive and our inner eyes were enlightened so we might behold the Prince of peace and follow where He leads.

For many years, our family lived in Northern California near the Pacific Ocean, and we were privileged to be able to visit the coast on a regular basis. The coastline contains numerous small, secluded beaches, rough surf and rocky cliffs. If you sit on a beach and look out over the water, you will see waves crashing and foaming about the tops of many rocks jutting above the surface.

One afternoon, as I sat and watched a rock as it was battered by the turbulent waves, I thought of Psalm 40:1-3: *He set my feet upon a rock and made my steps secure....* I chuckled and reflected that those rocks certainly didn't look as if they would provide secure footing!

Often our lives can feel as though we are trying to walk on slippery rocks, fearful of falling as waves pound all around us. When that happens, we call to mind that we have firm footing on the promises of Jesus, the Rock of our salvation. There are times a huge wave might come and take us by surprise and we feel that we lose our footing, but His word is secure and his presence is a strong foundation. Nothing happens that catches Him off-guard or escapes His notice. We do not depend on our ability to trust Him, but on His ability to set us upon the Rock and make our steps secure.

I feel as though the more I learn to trust my Savior, the ground becomes more spacious and level beneath my feet, so that I walk ever more securely without stumbling. But actually, the Rock I stand upon has always been spacious and secure. I just need to keep my eyes focused on Him. Where He leads, I follow; and He always guides me on paths of righteousness into green pastures where I am well-tended and secure.

As you journey through this day and encounter situations surrounded by unrest, you can maintain your sure footing in rest and trust by continuing to walk on the path of peace that comes from Jesus. He is taking us to the land of promise; do not follow the detours of fear, doubt, unrest, and confusion that beckon you, enticing you to turn aside for a moment. God grants us peace, and he also enables us to point to signs along the way, helping others to follow. We are carriers of salvation, hope and peace.

Daily Activation

Luke 1:76-79

"…for you will go on before the Lord to prepare the way for him, to give his people the knowledge of salvation through the forgiveness of their sins, because of the tender mercy of our God, by which the rising sun will come to us from heaven to shine on those living in darkness and in the shadow of death, to guide our feet into the path of peace."

Day Seventeen Declaration:

I declare that God has placed my feet upon the path of peace and I am the voice of peace every place I travel this day. I walk in light and in peace as I walk in salvation. The light of heaven is upon me as I travel this pathway, therefore light shines upon all those living in darkness. I declare that peace is upon my path, because I walk in salvation and in the tender mercies of God. As peace has been established in me through salvation, I will call out to those living in darkness and fear around me, telling them that they too may walk on the path of peace through salvation. Just like John the Baptist, I will be a voice that points the way to the path of peace to all those around me today and every day to come.

Day Eighteen

Pursue Peace!

People love to pursue something that they want. Whether it is a sports car, a designer purse, a new home, an exciting adventure, or a new relationship—the pursuit to fulfill their desire begins. They will save, work, dream and somehow find a way to gain their prize.

A young man in love pursues a young woman with undivided focus. Nothing can deter his desire. His longing for her will cause him to gain her affection at any cost. She fills his thoughts when awake and haunts his dreams. When will he see her? How can he be close to her?

Do you long for peace that way? Are you willing to pursue it like a lovesick young man?

I believe that one of the most effectual lies the enemy has told God's people is that true peace is unobtainable. We think we somehow have to muddle through life affected by the chaos of our age. *But that is a lie!* I know that my children grew up feeling peaceful. They were secure in the knowledge that they had a dad and mom who were protecting and providing for them and loving them day and night. Even when we were limited in what we could provide financially, they still experienced peace. God is unlimited in His ability to protect, provide and love His children. Why then are so many living in fear and anxiety?

We have already noted many times that a major key to possessing peace is trust. Yesterday we looked at trust in the promises of Jesus as the only real path to true and lasting peace. Finances can fluctuate with economic highs and lows, relationships can go through joys and sorrows, health can deteriorate unexpectedly; even the world around you can change in a moment's time. This makes it important to have your peace grounded in faith and trust in Him. Still, you might ask, "I belong to Jesus, and I do believe Him, but I am still plagued with worry. Why don't I have peace?"

Lack of peace often stems from mistrust in God's goodness and His commitment to fulfill His promises in our lives. This directly affects our health, our relationships, our success and our quality of life. We know that stress ages us and takes a toll on our physical, mental and emotional health, while peace produces life and vitality. The benefits of peace are wonderful and lasting, and they come to us when we are truly able to trust the Lord.

It is important to realize that this trust is not simply whipping ourselves into a falsely cheerful emotional state, and it is not blind denial of our circumstances. Many people live their lives in circumstances that are beyond their natural means or abilities for provision. This sort of lifestyle can cause a person to lose peace if they do not truly believe that God is their provider. But God does not ask anyone to begin a journey that He does not then make provision for them to finish. If a person does not have a deep conviction in his or her heart that this is true, life can be a very rough road. We must begin with humility, abandoning ourselves to a firm belief in God's truthfulness.

Now faith is the assurance (the confirmation, the title deed) of the things [we] hope for, being the proof of things [we] do not see and the conviction of their reality [faith perceiving as real fact what is not revealed to the senses] (Hebrews 11:1 AMP).

Our guarantee of eternal life is completely unseen by the human eye or comprehended by the human mind. Likewise, our guarantee of God's care throughout our earthly sojourn is also unseen. All of our assurances are faith based – unseen yet historically proven – but we can still have peace, because faith is our guarantee (assurance) of our hope.

You *can* find sure footing on the path to peace. Cry out to God for courage to trust Him with your whole heart, as you cast aside the temptation to lean on your own understanding (Proverbs 3:5-6). The pursuit of peace is a key to abundant living. It is found through intimacy and trust, and Jesus stands willing and able to draw you into His presence and teach you. Make your pursuit of Him deliberate and intentional; tell Him you want to live in the peace He has promised. He will be pleased by your obedience and your pursuit of His ways.

This is a new day, a day to pursue peace with humility and with zeal. *So let us strive for the things that bring peace and the things that build each other up* (Romans 14:19). If you are going to strive in anything, strive to enter into peace!

Daily Activation

Psalm 34:14

Turn from evil and do good; seek peace and pursue it.

Day Eighteen Declaration:

I declare over my life that I can and will obtain peace! I have begun my pursuit of living in God's peace and I will not stop until my life is lived in the boundaries of peace. Just as I pursue love, I will run after peace. Today I take the hand of my Prince of Peace and I will allow Him to lead me. His peace will become my peace just as His righteousness has become my righteousness. Thank you Jesus for the peace that you give to me as I accept your invitation into intimacy with you.

Day Nineteen

Peace Puts Satan under Your Feet

My first experience on a horse was not a positive one. My best friend was a very experienced rider, having won dozens of riding contests. I watched her ride for years and she made it look so easy. One day I got tired of watching and asked to ride, so she saddled up a horse and gave me some simple instructions. I was nervous but excited. As soon as I mounted her horse, it sensed my anxiety and began to pull to the left. My nervousness quickly turned into fear as the horse bucked aggressively and then ran off with me. I had no control, and the horse knew it.

I managed to hang on so I didn't fall and get trampled, but I was gripped by terror. Eventually, my friend's mom got into her vehicle and was able to trap the horse and stop him. When I asked why this horse could be so gentle and obedient to my best friend and so wild with me, my friend's mother said, "Horses sense fear and they will take advantage of the fearful rider. They also sense peace and will obey the peaceful and confident rider."

I have thought of this story many times as an adult when satan sought to take me on a wild ride. Many times I responded in fear, and the enemy sensed it and "took off" with me. But whenever I responded in peace and confidence in my God, I watched the enemy crushed under His mighty feet.

A few years ago the Lord spoke clearly to me:

Watch carefully, for the enemy is coming like a thief who will try to steal your peace. He is unleashing demonic assignments to exaggerate emotions and to bring forth vain imaginations that will try to exalt themselves above truth, wisdom, and the knowledge of God. His goal is to cause My people to move off the Rock of their peace so that they are vulnerable to being harmed during times of storms and shakings.

Over the next several months, as I prayed about this word I began to understand that when we allow fear to rule our thoughts and our actions, it actually creates fertile ground for the enemy to sow tares of doubt and fear, exaggerating and exacerbating difficult circumstances in our minds. This will cause our perspective of those circumstances to become warped. Additionally, satan probes for weaknesses in people's souls as he attempts to lure them into being led by their feelings, rather than by the Spirit. No one is ever immune from this assault. The enemy whispers lies in order to exaggerate situations so we will give way to an emotional reaction grounded in fear, rather than trust and perfect love.

The key to overcoming is to give the peace of Christ rulership in our hearts. On Day One, we looked at Paul's admonition in Colossians 3:15 to *"Let the peace of Christ rule in your hearts, since as members of one body you were called to peace. And be thankful."* Remember that when Jesus has His rightful place as King over our lives, we will be led by peace—the peace that surpasses all our human understanding. The rule of Christ is vital to the life of the believer; without it we open ourselves to an amazing amount of unnecessary emotional and spiritual turmoil.

God is in the process of strengthening His people so that they will live by the Spirit and respond to Him rather than react to the enemy's assignments against their fragile emotions. The Lord allows trials to exercise and strengthen our faith. The Bible teaches that our flesh will always try to gain the upper hand in our lives and cause us to react to circumstances with fear and unbelief. By God's grace we must let our spirits take charge over our flesh and cause us to submit to the rule of Christ, who will enable us to respond to challenges with grace, wisdom and peace.

We live in emotionally trying times. It is vital that we maintain awareness of what the Spirit is speaking to the Church, so we are not moved from our posture of truth and peace. When our feet and firmly planted on the Rock of truth that gives us peace, we are not readily swayed by imaginations that are not founded on God's words to us.

Just before He went to the cross, Jesus reminded His disciples that while they were in this world, they would face tribulation, but He went on to say "...be of good cheer, I have overcome the world." That promise is for you also. The Lord is with you today, and He has all authority to put the plans and schemes of the enemy under your feet. Walk sure-footedly, trusting in Him as He leads you continually into greater peace.

Daily Activation

Romans 16:20

The God of peace will soon crush Satan under your feet. The grace of our Lord Jesus be with you.

Day Nineteen Declaration:

I declare that my life is guarded by The God of peace. I place myself continually under the rule of His peace and protection. He will crush Satan under His feet as I put my trust in Him and do not fear. I will begin each day knowing that the God of peace is protecting me and will not allow the enemy to destroy me. I enter into His peace know that greater is He who is in me than he who is in the world.

Day Twenty

Reconciliation

My parents had not been believers during my childhood and their lives (and mine) were entangled by sin and shame. My parents and I gave our lives to Christ in my senior year of high school. We went through a time of counseling together and one day our therapist asked us to confess the sins that we committed against one another. One at a time, each of us wept and confessed our failures. With each confession the therapist would put a handful of tissues at our feet to represent the pain that had been caused. Before long each of us had a very large pile of tissues at our feet.

When we were finished confessing the therapist took the three piles of tissues and put them into one pile. Then he shared how Jesus took all of our sins upon Himself while dying on the cross so that we could be reconciled to Him. In that moment we felt the burden of our sins and shame lift from our lives. The sin had divided us but His blood reconciled us. The shame had divided us from experiencing the depths of His love but peace through His blood came to set us free.

Too often, many of us in the Church allow the accuser of the brethren to gain a foothold in our minds and hearts through offense that come when we sin against each other. The Lord does not want us to overlook sin, but the enemy is quick to take advantage of our weakness and foolishness, and he distracts us with accusations against others that take root in our heart and cause division in our ranks. We have all sinned and fallen short of His glorious standards, but in the Lord's merciful grace He has embraced us, forgiven us and restored us to Himself.

One of the most sobering parables Jesus ever told was the Parable of the Unmerciful Servant found in Matthew 18:21-35. Peter asked Jesus how often he has to forgive his brother or sister who sins against him. Jesus replied, "Seventy times seven." In other words, without limit. He then went on to relate the story of a servant freely forgiven by his master of an unpayable debt. This same servant then goes out from his master's presence and refuses to forgive one of his fellow servants a small debt. Jesus ended the parable:

"In anger, (the servant's) master turned him over to the jailers until he should pay back all he owed. This is how my heavenly Father will treat each of you unless you forgive your brother from your heart."

We are commanded to forgive from our hearts. We have been forgiven of so much; how can we clutch so ferociously to unforgiveness? We cannot truly know the peace of God if we cling to bitterness and offense. By no means am I promoting lawlessness, and I understand that there are people who have suffered incredible abuse and wickedness. Sometimes there are extreme situations where restoration of a relationship isn't possible. But for most of us, when we fail to extend to one another the grace freely extended to us by Jesus, we are in disobedience. He is able to create within us all the righteousness that God requires, but we must submit to His call to walk in forgiveness and restoration.

Not too long ago I saw a news story about a couple who were walking hand in hand when the young man was struck in the head by lightning. The electricity was transferred through his body, through both their hands, then down her body and out her feet. The doctors that treated them said that they were alive because they "shared the strike". Had the young man taken the full force on his own it most likely would have killed him, but because he was joined hand to hand with his girlfriend, neither of them was seriously injured.

This is a beautiful picture of unity and our need for one another. When we stand in opposition to each other, we cannot withstand the strikes of the enemy; but when we join in intimacy and unity we overcome.

We have all been wounded by others. My parents and I had sinned deeply and grievously against each other, and it was necessary to face what we had done, so that we could receive cleansing and forgiveness from Jesus and from each other. The process can be incredibly painful, but if you commit yourself to the path of forgiveness and healing, the Holy Spirit will make a way for you to find peace. The Lord is able to restore anything the enemy has stolen, as we receive and release mercy.

Today His blood still makes peace for you and reconciles you to live in the fullness of His love. You can live in peace because of the blood of Jesus.

Daily Activation

Colossians 1:19-20

For God was pleased to have all his fullness dwell in him, and through him to reconcile to himself all things, whether things on earth or things in heaven, by making peace through his blood, shed on the cross.

Day Twenty Declaration:

I declare the reconciliation that comes by making peace through His blood. I am at peace with my past, my present and my future because He has taken my sin and shame. I declare reconciliation of every area of my life by His blood. I declare the reconciliation of relationships that free all men from their shortcomings and sin. Peace and reconciliation are made through the shed blood of Jesus Christ and it is mine. Today I walk free from sin and shame because of the blood of the Lamb.

Day Twenty-one

Transcendent Peace

God has many traits that are beyond our natural understanding. Peace is one of those. Peace is a gift that is not easily understood by our minds. We have come far in this journey, and I pray by now you recognize some of the ways in your life you may have attempted to gain temporary peace, but have come to understand more fully the true gift of peace offered you by the Prince of Peace. Lasting peace transcends anything we can conceive through natural thinking.

I love early morning sunrises when it appears that the entire world around me is at peace. The birds are singing, warm sunlight brushes the treetops with brilliance, the air is crisp and everything feels new. This is peace that my mind can understand; it is also a peace that lasts but a moment. Soon the world awakens and demands begin and we need peace that transcends our understanding. Sunrise peace is wonderful but momentary; God's peace extends through the day and into the darkest part of night. This is the peace that we are breaking into.

This peace breaks through turmoil the way light dispels darkness; it breaks the stranglehold of anxiety; it comforts those who mourn and it makes a pathway through every difficulty that we face.

There have been many seasons in our family's life that the Lord has asked us to live completely by faith. The first time we did this was when we moved to another country to direct a house of prayer. We obeyed the Holy Spirit by leaving jobs, our church family, our relatives and our newly built home. We hadn't had time to raise financial support or to do much of anything beyond packing. We ended up living as prayer missionaries for many years with our four children, our animals, and our faith. The one thing that was often missing was my personal peace. I fretted with our posture of trusting God for every financial need, since we didn't have the promise of a guaranteed paycheck. I would spend days sick to my stomach before rent was due or when our bank account ran dry. God always came through, but I lost my peace in the process often.

Once again, we are in a time that God has called us to live without guaranteed income. The difference is that now I go to bed with peace, and wake up still peaceful. That is not to say that I NEVER have a moment of battling past what my eyes see, so I can reorient my emotions into what my spirit knows. Of course we all have those moments. But I have stopped relying on my understanding. Peace transcends understanding just as faith transcends sight. I know that God is faithful to supply and resource all He has asked us to do. I usually don't understand how He will supply our needs, but my peace is not in the "how" but in the Who. WHO HE IS has become the reason for my peace.

Paul wrote to the Philippians (and to us) to remind them not to be anxious about anything. Seriously? This seems to be an impossible injunction. There is much to be concerned about! But the apostle goes on to exhort us: ...*in everything, by prayer and petition, with thanksgiving, present your request to God* (Philippians 4:6). The key is that we put our trust fully in our good and gracious heavenly Father, who does all things well. We call out to Him, telling Him our concerns and thanking Him for answers He faithfully provides. He then gives His peace that surpasses all human reasoning, and this peace, like a sentinel, continually patrols and stands guard over all our emotions and our thoughts and wills.

If you struggle to maintain peace in the midst of impossibilities, you too can move into a peace that transcends your understanding by letting go of the "how" and embracing the "Who". Trust yourself and your circumstances into His loving and powerful hands. He is faithful. He will guard both your heart and your mind in Christ Jesus as you let go of the need to understand.

Daily Activation

Philippians 4:7

And the peace of God, which transcends all understanding, will guard your hearts and your minds in Christ Jesus.

Day Twenty-One Declaration:

Today I come into the peace that transcends my understanding. I have sought to find a way to obtain peace but it has not been lasting peace. I now receive the peace that comes from God alone. I declare that the peace of God is the only solution for my anxious heart. I receive this gift that I cannot understand with my mind but I can experience in my soul. I accept the peace of God that is spoken of in Philippians 4:7 that will guard my heart and my mind in Christ Jesus.

Day Twenty-two

Peace like a River

God spoke to the prophet Isaiah and promised to extend peace like a river to Jerusalem. For years, I never really understood how peace could be compared to a river. Rivers are often fast moving, and peace always seemed to me better compared to a placid, quiet body of water. Nevertheless, Isaiah says that Jerusalem's peace will be like a river.

One morning I awakened with this scripture portion on my mind, and asked the Lord how peace could be like a river. Immediately, I saw the days of my life as though they were a riverbed. Peace was an ever-moving, pure flow of water between the banks. The water moved swiftly, with purpose, and it provided a refreshing drink for anyone who came alongside me.

We often think of peace as stillness, but when we are filled with peace, it is tangible to others; it radiates from us and baptizes us with joy and strength. There is a washing of living water available for the people of God that will refresh every dry and stagnant place within. It is the movement of His peaceful life within us. The greater this flow of peace in our lives, the more it expands the boundaries of our "riverbed", saturating us and offering refreshment to people we encounter.

Ask the Father to wash you deeper in His peaceful presence this day, so that the river of His peace will pour upon you and flow through you in order to refresh you with new life. As you have postured yourself for breakthrough into greater peace these last few weeks, God will move on your behalf and not only give you triumph over the opposition you have faced, but will also awaken and revive you so you can go out in joy and peace. It His good pleasure and loving purpose that you are swept along joyfully by the waters of His river.

In God's living water, there is healing for pain that you have faced. Ask the Holy Spirit to continue to release your soul from trauma and discouragement as you are refreshed. He will release upon you that transcendent peace we discussed yesterday—peace that is beyond shameful memories, beyond your understanding, beyond your circumstances.

See, I am doing a new thing! Now it springs up; do you not perceive it? I am making a way in the desert and rivers in the wasteland (Isaiah 43:19). The LORD removes any obstacles before you as you journey toward His peace, clearing your pathway, and then He speaks to your "dry wastelands" and BEHOLD: there is water!

So, what is still before you today causing you to have anxiety in your heart? Allow the Holy Spirit to turn your anxiety into expectation. Peace purifies all that it touches and propels us forward. Peace is a pure stream of life that can cascade through us, healing our wounds. Take a deep breath and dive into this river, allowing the Holy Spirit to carry you to new adventures. As we are immersed in peace, we are able to offer the water of life to a desperate world thirsty for hope.

Daily Activation

Isaiah 66:12-13

For this is what the LORD says: "I will extend peace to her like a river, and the wealth of nations like a flooding stream; you will nurse and be carried on her arm and dandled on her knees. As a mother comforts her child, so will I comfort you; and you will be comforted over Jerusalem."

Day Twenty-two Declaration:

I declare that from this day on I will have peace like a river. Peace will cause forward movement in my life, it will bring me strength will purify my life. I will be a source of fresh water to all those who stand at the riverbank of my life. As I have peace, they too will receive peace. Peace is not passive; it is strong and floods every part of me. I receive the floodwaters of peace to immerse my life and to saturate every dry place. Peace will expand my borders and add strength to move me forward. I receive the comfort and refreshing that peace adds to my life. I will no longer only look for peace in the stillness but I now receive the flow of peace that comes like a river.

Day Twenty-three

Peace in Action

What do you do when you hear of an urgent need of someone around you? You may not be able to solve their entire problem but you might be able to bring them peace by helping meet some or all of their physical need. James warns us against becoming the type of people who look at someone in need and say, "Go in peace, be warm and be filled" and then go our way without doing anything to meet the need. Peace is hard to obtain in the midst of physical lack and desperate need. If we want people to "go in *peace*" then we need to do what we can to be a *piece* of the solution.

I believe that when we personally involve ourselves in the need of another person, we both give peace and we gain peace. The other person moves on in peace, having been helped, and we can go in peace knowing that we were the help that they needed.

One morning I was headed to a local grocery store to grab a few items. As I pulled into the parking lot, the Holy Spirit stopped me and said, *"I want you to withdraw $100 in cash before you go into the store because someone is in need of it."*

I withdrew the money and then walked into the store asking Holy Spirit to direct me. As I walked the aisles praying, I noticed a man and woman pushing a grocery cart. I immediately sensed the Spirit quicken to me that they were to be the recipients of the money.

I walked to the next aisle and saw the couple standing in front of the toilet paper products. They were in the middle of a discussion, but I excused myself and asked if I could share something with them. They seemed troubled and distracted, but they were polite and told me to go ahead.

I began by explaining that I was a Christian and before coming into the store I sensed God asked me to get money out of the ATM, because there was someone in need inside the store. At that point their eyes widened and I could tell I had their full attention.

Then I told them how, when I saw them, God told me they were the ones who were supposed to receive the funds. I handed the man $100 and as he took it from my hand he began to weep. He started to tell me how he and his wife had just been arguing, because they needed both toilet paper and milk for their children, but only had enough money for one item. He said they actually needed far more than that, but they had decided to choose what was needed most and were about to get the toilet paper.

He went on to say that while they stood, staring at the different options, he thought, "Maybe we shouldn't stay together because this is not working and she would be better off without me."

At that moment I showed up and not only offered more help than they needed financially, but showed him that God was for his marriage and family. The man dropped to his knees right in the middle of the grocery store aisle and began to thank God for this miracle: for saving him from leaving his family and for showing His provision in their time of need.

Chaos had filled this man's heart. The burden of lack, of failure, and the great responsibility of being a husband and a father had stolen all his peace. But our great Peacemaker sent me to restore peace to his heart and to stop a decision that would have broken up a family. God is not only our peace, but He uses willing sons and daughters to be those who bring peace wherever they go.

Most of us have given to those in need, as well as received from someone else in our time of need. When our needs are met we walk in much greater peace. We must be willing to be His hands and feet to people around us who are in need. It can often be as simple as just being available to someone who is hurting. You have no idea how Jesus may use you, or the importance of your "small" acts of kindness.

You may not be able to help everyone in every need, but as much as possible, put your peace in action so that it is passed onto another. Peace is tangible expression as well as calm assurance. You will gain peace as you bring peace to others. Freely and generously give and you will generously receive.

Daily Activation

James 2:16

If one of you says to them, "Go in peace; keep warm and well fed," but does nothing about their physical needs, what good is it?

Day Twenty-three Declaration:

I am the hands and feet of Jesus! As I go through my day I will be sensitive to hear the Holy Spirit and respond when He shows me a need that I can help fulfill. I declare that my life will not be marked merely by words of faith but by faith in action. I will pass the peace that You have given me along to others so that they can experience peace in the midst of their storm. When I am able to do so I will not only speak a blessing, but I will be a blessing to someone in need. They will "go in peace" because I am willing to bring them peace in action. I am no longer only seeking peace for my life but I am seeking peace to give to others. This day I move into a greater expression of peace in action.

Day Twenty-four

Bless Where You Are

There are times in our lives that we don't particularly like where we live, where we work or even who we are living with. Learning to bless where the Lord has placed you and who He has placed you with is key to your peace and prosperity.

If a city or nation suffers, the people suffer. Praying for peace and prosperity upon your city and nation is like praying for peace and prosperity upon your own life. When it thrives, the people thrive. The same is true for your work place. If your work place is a place of oppression, anxiety and poverty then the people who work there will experience those very things. As you pray for peace and prosperity in your work place (or your spouse's work place), you will surely get the overflow of this transformation.

What about your home and the people that you live with, such as parents or roommates? If you are married with a family, do you continually bless your spouse and children, even during those days you find it difficult to get along with them? As you daily pray for their peace and prosperity and watch them breakthrough, it will result in a greater breakthrough into your personal peace. Even if you take just one minute a day to pray for them, it may be the most important minute of your daily routine.

Too often it is easy to focus on negatives. We find all sorts of reasons to be critical of others, or avoid people because there is just "something about them" that we do not like. Petty annoyances inflate into overwhelming conflicts and divisions when we fix our attention on criticism. The accuser of the brethren is only too happy to add fuel to any of these types of fires we want to burn. There is a reason that the enemy works so hard to divide individuals, especially in the Body of Christ. It is because we need one another so very much. The Lord knows this and that is why throughout Scripture we are exhorted to encourage one another.

Even Jesus, during His night when He was betrayed, longed for His disciples. Just knowing that they were awake and keeping watch with Him would have brought Him great comfort. Let us not be asleep in the hour of need that many brothers and sisters are facing or will face in the days to come.

Now is the time to nurture the relationships and connections that the Lord has given you within His Body. Find out where the Lord desires to plant you and then grow there. Our Lord Jesus surrounded Himself with intimate relationships during His time on earth. God still desires companionship with us, His chosen and beloved ones. We who are in the Body of Christ are the only ones that know the plans of the Father. His plans are the truth that will carry us through, and we must be encouragers of each other, calling each other up to the fullness God prepared for us. Speak peace and the manifestation of God's destiny to the people and the places where you live and work.

Daily Activation

Jeremiah 29:7

Also, seek the peace and prosperity of the city to which I have carried you into exile. Pray to the LORD for it, because if it prospers, you too will prosper."

Day Twenty-four Declaration:

God, I declare peace and prosperity over my nation, my city, my work place, my home and my family. I speak the peace that comes from God over each of these places and all of these people. I declare that you are establishing peace in the government of my city and nation. I declare that you are establishing peace in those in authority at my work place. I pray that you would give your wisdom to all those in authority in government, business and church leadership. I declare your peace over every person in my family. Release your wisdom upon them for every decision that they make throughout this day. I declare peace into their souls and upon their paths today. My life will be surrounded by peace and prosperity as spoken of in Jeremiah 29:7.

Day Twenty-five

Honor and Unity

An important aspect of walking in wholeness and peace is to be able to journey in healthy relationships with others. All of us who have been born again through trust in Christ Jesus have become part of His Body, and therefore we are dependent on one another. We each function with different gifts and talents, so we have different roles to fulfill. The importance of unity, working together as one without jostling one another, is vital. Just as my hand depends on the proper function of my arm in order to be fully effective, so I am dependent upon the other members of Christ's Body to function in my gift properly.

The Lord is joining the members of His body like never before. He is restoring us as family and knitting our hearts together in love as we are being prepared for the days ahead. The various gifts and callings among His people are becoming clearer, and He is releasing greater wisdom for us to know how they work together. Every gift is equally important.

Do not think of yourself more highly than you ought, but rather think of yourself with sober judgment, in accordance with the measure of faith God has given you. Just as each of us has one body with many members, and these members do not all have the same function, so in Christ we who are many form one body, and each member belongs to all the others (Romans 12:3-5).

My natural family works together so well because each person contributes his or her part. Jeff and I have one child who has amazing discernment, another who is a visionary, another who nurtures and protects; and so on. We trust one another and honor each person's particular gifts. The children understand their dad's strengths and their mom's strengths and how we each function. The same way, we learn how to discern each other's abilities in the Body of Christ, so we can honor one another and bless how each member functions. We no longer live in an age where just one or two individuals lead with vision and the rest follow to support the work of a few. We all are called to advance the Kingdom, living and working as family.

One Body, many members. This is part of God's holy alignment as He purifies His family and brings us into harmony and peace with each other. We must learn to honor and cherish every gift; from the one who serves to the one who prophesies to the one who exercises oversight. Honoring one another as equal and vital to the whole is breaking cycles of conflict and misunderstanding that in past years has left many people feeling unimportant and forsaken. Unity and dependency are like a two-edged sword. It is the truth revealed to His sons and daughters who live in a world that tries to deceive us into living apart from Him and one another. As we learn to love and esteem one another, we are fulfilling the prayer of Jesus in John 17 that we would be one as He and the Father are one. This brings blessing and peace and enables us to show the glory of God to our world which desperately needs salvation.

Recently the Lord told a dear friend of ours, "Honor breaks the curse." She realized that curses of separation, of division and orphan spirits are broken as we give and receive honor. This is a principle of God's Kingdom: Give and you will receive, bless and you will be blessed, honor and you will be honored. We all find ourselves in conflict with others at times, but if we focus on the value of each person, and commit our hearts to living in humility and forbearance, we will discover joy and peace that brings wisdom from the Lord and helps us to "dwell together in unity," which releases blessing on us all (see Psalm 133). More importantly, as we live in peace with one another, we honor and bless our King of kings, who paid the ultimate price that we would be made one in Him.

We need each other. "No man is an island entire of itself" wrote John Dunne almost 400 years ago, and that is still true today. My area of weakness may be your area of strength and my strength may be your weakness, and together we can hold one another up as God holds us all. We were not created to live independently from one another or from God. The Father earnestly longs for His entire family to walk in the precious blessing of unity. Let's walk in peace with one another and fulfill His dream!

Daily Activation

Ephesians 4:2-3

Be completely humble and gentle; be patient, bearing with one another in love. Make every effort to keep the unity of the Spirit through the bond of peace.

Day Twenty-five Declaration:

Father, I declare today that I walk in humility, and understand my part as Your beloved child. I join myself to You and to the members of the body of Christ, recognizing that we all hold a cherished place in Your heart, and we all have a part to play in Your great adventure of the Kingdom. I am dependent on You and on my brothers and sisters. I honor their callings and gifts, even as I gratefully acknowledge the gifts You have placed within me. I choose peace in my interactions with others; I will speak blessings of honor as I make every effort to remain in unity with others, and call forth the unique treasure hidden within each individual. This honor breaks curses of disunity and bitterness. I declare favor on my loved ones, favor on my brothers and sisters in Christ, and favor on my own life as well. I walk in peace today, because I "make every effort" to walk in unity that brings blessing.

Day Twenty-six

Becoming a Peacemaker

As God's people we long for His wisdom to guide us through life and every decision that we face. In James 3:17-18 we read that wisdom from heaven has certain characteristics that become a part of who we are. Peace is just one of those characteristics; others are that it is pure, loving, considerate, submissive (obedient), merciful, fruitful, impartial and sincere. These characteristics, when received into our lives, cause us to be peacemakers who have the opportunity to sow in peace and reap a harvest of righteousness.

If these characteristics cause us to become peacemakers then they cause us to walk in peace as well. Begin to intentionally focus on these traits and declare them over your life. As you do this you will not only reap peace but a "harvest of righteousness" as well.

Our words are far more powerful than some of us realize. We possess delegated authority as Christ's representatives, and our declarations are expressions of faith—whether positive or negative. Words can heal and release profound blessing, but they can also wound and harm. When we align every word that comes from our mouths with God's heart, we change the spiritual "atmosphere" around us and release blessings on the people around us. Likewise, if we allow ourselves to mutter and complain and criticize—even if it is quietly— we release negativity that affects others. The people of God are called to be salt and light in the world, and our words should also be those that preserve peace and bring hope.

Jesus said what flows from our mouth pours forth from the abundance of our hearts (Matthew 12:33-35). Once words are released from our mouths, we can't reach out and stuff them back in! It's like firing a gun—once the trigger is pulled, we can't stop the bullet from hitting the target at which it was aimed. If we have spoken harshly in a moment of frustration or bitterness, we may regret what we said, but damage has been done. That is why Scripture tells us to be quick to listen and slow to speak. We can ask the Holy Spirit to continually renew our minds, transforming our lives so that we are aligned with His character. In that way, our words will release peace and blessing, affirming wholeness and God's truth.

There is one whose rash words are like sword thrusts, but the tongue of the wise brings healing (Proverbs 12:18). It is important that we come into agreement with all God says about ourselves, our families, our friends and those around us we may interact with. Asking God for the tongue of a wise man is wisdom! Wisdom speaks life and healing. Ask God to align every word that comes from your mouth with His heart. Let your conversations be seasoned with life and love.

Begin today to choose words that are pleasing to the Lord. We want our speech to give grace and peace to everyone who hears us. Proverbs 18:21 declares, *Death and life are in the power of the tongue, and those who love it will eat its fruits.* This is wonderful fruit indeed, sweetened with life and truth. Healing words, soothing words, words that build up and release peace; these are pleasing to Jesus. Start your mornings by praying and declaring words of hope and life over yourself and your family. Then as you go about your day, look for opportunities to release peace into the lives of those you encounter through your words and your deeds.

Pray the passage from James below, and meditate on the reality that when you ask God for His wisdom you are asking Him for so much more than just an answer. Yesterday we declared honor and unity; today you are asking Him to place within you all the traits that make you a peacemaker. I declare life and purity over you this day! Release the peace you have on a troubled world that needs it so desperately.

Daily Activation

James 3:17-18

But the wisdom that comes from heaven is first of all pure; then peace-loving, considerate, submissive, full of mercy and good fruit, impartial and sincere. Peacemakers who sow in peace reap a harvest of righteousness.

Day Twenty-six Declaration:

Father, I declare that I am on the journey to becoming a peacemaker. I receive Your wisdom and all the characteristics of Your wisdom. I sow into peace and reap a harvest of righteousness. I ask that my words will bring healing, life and peace to all those I live with and everyone I meet. I walk in the wisdom that comes from heaven so that I will carry peace, produce peace and sow peace.

Day Twenty-seven

Peace: The Reward for Obedience

Leviticus 26 is a chapter that focuses on the "Reward for Obedience". When we decide to obey the Lord and leave behind every place of stubborn rebellion in our life, there is a reward promised to us.

Just as a young child is rewarded by their parents for good behavior and for acting responsibly; so our Heavenly Father is quick to reward His obedient children. Why do we reward? It is to say, "Well done!" Good behavior keeps our children safe, blessed and full of our favor. Obeying the voice and commandments of our God keep us safe in His blessings and overshadows our lives with His favor.

Our oldest son was a very obedient child. When he was young he would occasionally approach me and inform me that he needed to be disciplined. I was always surprised (and inwardly tickled) by this; even though he was genuinely remorseful, from my perspective his confession was usually about something pretty trivial. But I was grateful for his tender heart and his honesty and I was happy to forgive, rarely feeling the need for much discipline. Restoration of relationship was more important at this point. I was fairly confident that he had been sitting in his room feeling badly that he had done something that offended his conscience, recognizing that his parents—and God—would not approve of his actions. His confession and request for discipline came at the end of the wrestle with his sensitive conscience. What happened in these moments was that he gained greater trust from us, his parents. Whether he had directly disobeyed a command, or done something that violated his conscience, his desire for obedience and confession brought a reward. Even though there was a temptation to hide the offense, especially when I didn't know about it, he preferred the blessings of peace that came from a clean conscience and restoration.

Because he was continually obedient, we extended him a reward of trust that gave him more freedom than if he had been a disobedient child. The same is true for us. When our Heavenly Father sees that He can trust us with obedience then we are rewarded with greater authority, more freedom and opportunities to receive His favor. As a parent, it gives me much greater pleasure to reward than to restrict.

Let us be children that bring joy to God's heart by making opportunities for Him to reward us. Through the power of the Holy Spirit, He has provided the means for us to obey Him (Romans 7:25-8:4; Galatians 5:16-18). Read the promises granted to God's obedient servants in Leviticus 26; they are wonderful. One of the promises is peace! He promises that we will lie down in safety and not be afraid. As you obey His voice, He promises that you can lie down in peace. Too many of God's people still end their days anxious with all the worries of the past and concerns about the days to come, rather than falling asleep quietly in God's peace.

Tonight, lie down knowing that as you have walked in His commandments, you are protected by His promise and surrounded by His peace. You can sleep knowing that you are covered in His promised reward.

Daily Activation

Leviticus 26:6

I will grant peace in the land, and you will lie down and no one will make you afraid. I will remove wild beasts from the land, and the sword will not pass through your country.

Psalm 85:8

I will listen to what God the LORD will say; he promises peace to his people, his saints—but let them not return to folly.

Day Twenty-seven Declaration:

I declare today that I will walk in all of your commandments and will obey your voice. I will follow your decrees and be careful to obey your commands. I move into complete trust that your Spirit will make your will and your ways known to me. I receive correction as a loved child and ask that you would align my steps with your ways. I receive all of your rewards for obedience. I receive all the promises found in Leviticus 26 that are given as rewards for obedience. These promises are mine. I receive fruitfulness, provision, favor, victories over my enemies, increase and abundance. I also receive your peace. Tonight I will lie down in peace because you have promised me victory.

Day Twenty-eight

Out of Bounds

"Out of bounds" is the term used in sports when a team moves outside the boundaries of their playing field. Whenever I allow myself to move into fear, I ask the Holy Spirit to blow His whistle and declare, "Out of bounds!" Then I can quickly move back into the safety of trust and reliance upon His grace and goodness.

It is vital to embrace the truth of His unfailing love so that we may live in the boundaries of His peace. Scripture tells us *"There is no fear in love; instead, perfect love drives out fear…"* (1 John 4:18).

Peace has become a compass for me; if I am in peace then I am confident that I am walking in truth and complete dependency upon my Father God's promises to me. This is victory over the enemy of my soul. When I begin to fret and fear, I know that I have left the boundaries of peace that He has ordained to surround my life and walked into my own carnal strength and thoughts. Fear grips my heart as a result of focusing on worries and cares, but peace is my reward for trust.

Our adversary continually tempts us to fear so we will make decisions outside of God's truth and wisdom, and act out of our own understanding. Don't allow yourself to be enslaved by the demands and limitations of the world's systems. God's sons and daughters were not created to live according to the social and economic demands around us, but to dwell joyfully in the realm of His glorious Kingdom.

Our loving Father gives us room to run, explore, and seek adventure within the boundaries of His limitless love. Inside these lines of trust and peace we cease to live as individuals who react to circumstances, but rather become those who respond to Holy Spirit's leading. Our spirits come alive and begin to soar as we behold the miraculous and experience abundant living.

We have examined many wonderful promises of peace and looked at some of the ways God grants us peace. Jesus, the Prince of Peace, continually beckons us to *"Come, follow Me"* so we may dwell within His boundaries. Let us run after Him together. His presence is the promise and the reality of deliverance from all that oppresses us. The great preacher Charles Spurgeon commented: "Even to the boundaries quiet extends; no enemies are wrangling with the borderers. If there is peace there, we may be sure that peace is everywhere."

Commit today to always put your hope in the unfailing love of the One who builds protecting boundaries of peace for us. He will not disappoint! He will give peace to you, your family and all those who dwell in your gates.

Daily Activation

Psalm 16:5-6

LORD, you have assigned me my portion and my cup; you have made my lot secure. The boundary lines have fallen for me in pleasant places; surely I have a delightful inheritance.

Psalm 147:14

He grants peace to your borders and satisfies you with the finest of wheat.

Day Twenty-eight Declaration:

I declare that I will walk within the boundaries of the Lord all the days of my life. I commit my plans and my steps to the order of the Holy Spirit. Keep my life within your will and your plans. I choose trust, faith and Godly wisdom as my guide and peace as my compass. I will be one who responds to Your Spirit regardless of my circumstances and I reject an anxious spirit that causes me to react in fear. I receive Your peace and your wisdom, God. I will go forth in peace and in Your approval in my life's journey.

Day Twenty-nine

The Perspective of Peace

Perspective always has an impact upon a person's viewpoint—for instance, when we form an opinion about an issue, we generally base our thoughts on our opinions, beliefs and experiences. It is important that we don't view our lives through the distortions that can be caused by disappointments or difficult circumstances or fear. Even though we might think or feel that something is true, we must seek God's perspective and ask Him to give us His view of any situation.

I learned a valuable lesson about this the year my mother died. She had been sick for some time, and doctors didn't seem to know exactly what was wrong. Late one afternoon I received a call that she was in the hospital, having suddenly become critically ill. Within a few hours I was boarding a flight from San Francisco to my parent's home in Georgia. My dad and my siblings and I spent several exhausting and very bittersweet days at my mom's bedside, praying with her as she slipped in and out of consciousness. Mom went home to be with the Lord on Good Friday, holding my hand as she left us. That Easter Sunday would have been my parents' 51st wedding anniversary.

Over the next several days, we spent countless hours planning her memorial service and burial. Family arrived from different parts of the country to comfort us and to say their good-byes. By the time all the planning and arranging of schedules and services had been concluded, we were emotionally and physically spent. My dad decided he did not want to be at his house the day after his wife's funeral, so he left to spend the night at my brother's home about thirty miles away. I chose to stay at my parent's house to rest, along with my oldest son and his girlfriend, who both attended university in the area. However, this was not to be a restful day.

In the morning, we began to receive reports of severe weather—thunderstorms, strong winds and hail. We turned on the television and watched weather updates that revealed one storm cell after another headed directly our way, warning that they would last throughout the day and night.

I was born and raised in earthquake country in California, so I was used to predictions about catastrophes that might happen but did not come to pass. However, in this case, I realized we should be prepared, so we gathered supplies and continued to monitor all news reports. Over the next several hours, gigantic storms raged through our area. I had never seen the entire blackened sky come to touch the ground and then swirl the way we were seeing. It was frightening, but I became even more fearful when the reports changed from talking about severe thunder and hail to warning about tornados.

Not only had I never been in a tornado, but what I was seeing reported was an unprecedented number of tornados, and our town was one of the areas directly in their path. The kids and I quickly collected flashlights, batteries, a transistor radio, blankets and water. As we moved downstairs, a local radio station announced that a mile-wide tornado with winds up to 175 miles per hour was headed straight towards us.

My son's girlfriend, Brittany, had lived in the south for a number of years and had faced a number of these warnings. She was calm and peaceful through the entire ordeal. My son had only been living in the south for a year, so this was all new to him—and to me. We knew what to do in an earthquake: curl up for protection under a large object; but we were pretty sure that was not going to protect us from a huge tornado!

Soon after retreating to the basement, the electricity went out and the winds began to howl. The lightning was like nothing I'd ever seen before. There were no intervals between strikes. I was frightened, but Brittany sat peacefully as if she were just waiting for the sun to rise. The announcer on the radio then reported that the tornado had just hit downtown Ringgold and many businesses were gone.

Finally, after many hours we received a phone text from my brother telling us that the last storm cell had passed and we could safely move back upstairs. We emerged from the basement and the kids fell asleep on the living room couches. I sat in the dark, and realized an eerie calm had descended on the city. The darkness was like a physical weight, and suffocating fear like I've rarely known wrapped itself around me. I had been scared during the storms, but this was far beyond that. I was terrified beyond reason. Somehow I was able to access a phone line and place a phone call to Jeff in California. When he answered I told him to watch the Weather Channel and find out if any more tornados were coming my way, because we had lost even radio reception at this point. I was in the dark and cut off from all official communications. What if my brother's text had been wrong and another tornado was approaching?

Jeff immediately turned to national weather bulletins, and assured me that the last storm cell had passed over our area and was headed toward Atlanta, Georgia. I kept saying, "Are you sure? Are you sure?" He told me he would continue to watch and call me if conditions changed. About two a.m. I finally fell asleep for a few hours. When I awoke we discovered that much of the city had been destroyed, and that over 150 tornados had touched down in those few hours taking over 300 lives. Huge tornados had missed my parent's home by a little over a mile.

Though I was scared during the worst parts of the storms, the gripping fear that hit me like a freight train came after all the danger had left. However, because I didn't know for sure what was happening, I succumbed to a spirit of fear that hit me to keep me from finding peace when the calm came.

The enemy will come like a thief during traumatic times to steal your hope. When this happens, it is vital that we find a way to gain God's perspective of our situation. Do not let fear overtake you, but reach out the Lord or to someone you trust who can speak truth and bring you back to your senses. For me, that was my husband. I knew that he would not put my life in danger but he would only tell me that which he was absolutely sure of. He not only watched national weather reports, but did online searches and looked at many different sources before assuring me that I was safe and could rest. Because he had a perspective different than mine, based on the truth about my circumstances, his encouragement silenced the voice of fear that night and brought me peace.

In the same way, God can give us understanding how to gain His perspective as He trains us to see with spiritual eyes, and hear with spiritual ears. According to Hebrews 12:2, the Lord is the author and finisher of our faith. He is the one who can take the turmoil of the huge storms in our lives and calm them restoring us to perfect peace.

Whether it is today or a day yet to come, you are sure to face stormy trials. But in every difficulty, the Holy Spirit is ready and willing to speak His wisdom, so that we would gain His perspective and trust in His provision and deliverance.

Daily Activation

James 1:5

If any of you lacks wisdom, he should ask God, who gives generously to all without finding fault, and it will be given to him.

Day Twenty-nine Declaration:

I declare this day that you, Jesus, are the author and finisher of my faith as written in Hebrews 12:2. You have the final word about every aspect of my life. You have complete wisdom regarding every storm that comes upon my life. I trust you to help me understand that wisdom when I ask you about the things I face. I know that you love me and will guide me into Your perspective, which allows me to move forward in peace. Grant me eyes to see, that I might view the days of my life from Your perspective. Help me to stay focused on You, Jesus, even as You rebuke the storms in my life and continually restore me to Your peace.

Day Thirty

Peace That Remains

It is day thirty! You have been building a foundation of peace over the past month. Although this book is not intended to guarantee that you will never experience fear, anxiety or stress again it is intended to establish a foundation of peace and a habit of pursuing true peace. You now have tools and a Biblical base for living in the benefits that peace brings into your life.

This book is just one of the tools that can be pulled out and read on days that challenge your peace. Speak the declarations over yourself and your family; better still, write your own, and declare them continually in faith. God desires for you to live in the fullness of His lasting peace. One of the key themes in this book is the truth that peace is not circumstantial, but instead results from an unshakeable trust in the goodness and faithfulness of our Father. His peace is readily available to you each and every day. It is a gift we can possess by believing. Jesus promised us in John 14:27, *"Peace I leave with you; my peace I give you. I do not give to you as the world gives. Do not let your hearts be troubled and do not be afraid."*

God is assuring you that you do not have to live a life ruled by a troubled heart; He has invited you into His peace. He is assuring you that you can confidently trust him with every aspect of your life. Peace is a direct result of confident trust and joy is a direct result of peace. You have begun a wonderful and exciting journey of living the way

God intended you to live.

When pain and trouble come, some may look at your situation and think, "Boy, I'm glad that isn't me!" People who could help you might even turn away and say, "It's not my problem." But, Jesus has a different message for you. He wants you to know that He identifies completely with you. He reminds you that your problem is not *your* problem but His! He gladly takes your troubled waters and exchanges them for the living water of His peace. You can be at peace because God, the Holy Spirit, is present with you at all times, your Counselor and Comforter who leads you into all truth.

The prince of this world is the thief of peace. He comes to steal, kill and destroy but he has no authority over the Prince of Peace who lives within you; therefore the enemy has no hold upon you either. The Savior's peace is your peace. The world cannot understand the peace that you have been given. It is not understood or experienced outside of salvation and receiving the Holy Spirit into your life. This peace is lasting peace; it cannot be stolen, lost or separated from you. Remain in truth and you will remain in peace.

You were created to live in peace. I often wonder if our lives would be greatly prolonged if we lived in the peace that we were created for. Stress and anxiety are symptoms of a life lived separated from trusting God and following His commandments. When Adam and Eve did the one thing that God asked them not to do, a separation and independence was formed. They had to learn to live outside of the garden and stress entered into the life of the human race. When Jesus died on the cross and then ascended to the Father, leaving us peace through His blood, we were reconciled to a life of peace. Now is the time to live in the truth that God has provided for us. Today is the first day of the rest of your life.

I leave you with this benediction from the Apostle Peter:

Peter, an apostle of Jesus Christ, to God's elect, strangers in the world...who have been chosen according to the foreknowledge of God the Father, through the sanctifying work of the Spirit, to be obedient to Jesus Christ and sprinkled with his blood: Grace and peace be yours in abundance (1 Peter 1:1-2).

Daily Activation

Day Thirty Declaration:

I declare that I was created to live in peace. Today I choose to live in confident trust that the Father, Son and Holy Spirit (My Advocate) will never leave me nor forsake me; therefore, I can receive His peace. God has given me a foundation of peace and I will daily pursue a life continually refreshed by peace and joy. When anxiety or fear knocks on the door of my life I will quickly run into the arms of my Prince of Peace who, according to Psalm 139:5, keeps me hemmed in before and behind.

I declare Psalm 121:7-8 over my life today and over all my days yet to come: The LORD will keep (me) from all harm—he will watch over (my) life; the LORD will watch over (my) coming and going both now and forevermore.

Amen.

Sources

Introduction
"peace, prosperity, health....": R. Laird Harris, Gleason L. Archer, Jr., Bruce K. Waltke (Eds.), *Theological Wordbook of the Old Testament, Vol. II* (Chicago: Moody Press, 1980), 931.

Day Seven: Breaking Every Chain
"We must keep in mind....": A.W. Tozer, *The Knowledge of the Holy* (New York: Harper & Row, 1961), 102.

Day Nine: Living in the Moment
"Worry does not empty....": Corrie Ten Boom. Retrieved from Goodreads.com. **https://www.goodreads.com/author/quotes/102203.Corrie_ten_ Boom**

Day Twelve: Be Still
"This quiet rest....": Richard J. Foster, *Streams of Living Water* (San Francisco: HarperCollins, 1998), 49.

Day Twenty-eight: Out of Bounds
"Even to the boundaries....": Charles H. Spurgeon, *The Treasury of David, Vol. III* (Peabody, Massachusetts: Hendrickson Publishers), 418.

Made in the USA
Charleston, SC
25 April 2016